D1626476

PILGRIM DAYS

OSPREY
PUBLISHING

We are the Pilgrims, master; we shall go
Always a little further; it may be
Beyond that last blue mountain barred with snow
Across that angry or that glimmering sea
White on a throne or guarded in a cave
There lies a prophet who can understand
Why men were born: but surely we are brave,
Who take the Golden Road to Samarkand.

These evocative lines have become synonymous with the Special Air Service (SAS). But they first originated in the words of the play *HASSAN – The Story of Hassan of Baghdad and how he came to make the Golden Journey to Samarkand* by James Elroy Flecker (1884–1915).

PILGRIM DAYS

FROM VIETNAM TO THE SAS

ALASTAIR MACKENZIE

I'd like to have two armies: one for display with lovely guns, tanks, little soldiers, staffs, distinguished and doddering Generals, and dear little regimental officers who would be deeply concerned over their General's bowel movements or their Colonel's piles, an army that would be shown for a modest fee on every fairground in the country.

The other would be the real one, composed entirely of young enthusiasts in camouflage uniforms, who would not be put on display, but from whom impossible efforts would be demanded and to whom all sorts of tricks would be taught. That's the army in which I should like to fight.

The Centurions by Jean Paul Lartéguy, translated by Xan Fielding, 1968

This book is dedicated to the people who have assisted me in my journey as a 'Pilgrim' following Odin, the God of War.

At the top of the list is my dearest wife, Cecilia, who died in September 2007. She was my guide and my 'rock' who came with me on the journey, raising our children, Juliette and Andrew, while I confronted the demons of war.

I also dedicate this book to all the centurions who fought alongside me – Kiwis, Parachute Regiment 'Toms', SAS 'blades', South African Parabats and Omani Jebalis as well as my colleagues in the cut-throat world of commerce.

This book is also dedicated to Nannette who helped pick up the pieces.

My father was a warrior, I was a warrior and my son is a warrior – this is my story.

OSPREY PUBLISHING
Bloomsbury Publishing Plc
PO Box 883, Oxford, OX1 9PL, UK
1385 Broadway, 5th Floor, New York, NY 10018, USA
E-mail: info@ospreypublishing.com
www.ospreypublishing.com

OSPREY is a trademark of Osprey Publishing Ltd

First published in Great Britain in 2019
© Alastair MacKenzie, 2019

A catalogue record for this book is available from the British Library.

ISBN: HB 9781472833181; eBook 9781472833174; ePDF 9781472833167; XML 9781472833150

19 20 21 22 23   10 9 8 7 6 5 4 3 2 1

Index by Zoe Ross
Typeset by Deanta Global Publishing Services, Chennai, India
Printed and bound in Great Britain by CPI (Group) UK Ltd, Croydon CR0 4YY

Front cover:
Main: the author on operations in Vietnam. (Author's Collection)
Background: A soldier looks for roadside bombs during a British armoured patrol in County Fermanagh, close to the border with the Republic of Ireland, 1978. (Photo by Alex Bowie/Getty Images)
Back cover flap:
Author's collection.

All photographs in the plates are from the author's personal collection.

Editor's note:
Imperial or metric measurements (or sometimes a combination) have been used in accordance with common usage in the various armies with which the author served. Likewise the names of units are rendered in accordance with the convention of that organisation.

Author's note:
Surnames of members of Special Forces and British armed forces personnel serving in Northern Ireland have been removed for political and legal reasons.

Osprey Publishing supports the Woodland Trust, the UK's leading woodland conservation charity.

To find out more about our authors and books visit www.ospreypublishing.com. Here you will find extracts, author interviews, details of forthcoming events and the option to sign up for our newsletter.

CONTENTS

GLOSSARY

Adoo	Enemy (Oman)
ANZAC	Australian and New Zealand Army Corps
AO	Area of operations
APC	Armoured personnel carrier
BAe	British Aerospace
BRA	Bougainville Resistance Army
CO	Commanding officer
CSM	Company sergeant major
CT	Counterterrorism
DCM	Distinguished Conduct Medal
doppie	Cartridge case (Afrikaans)
DPM	Disruptive pattern material
DSIR	Department for Scientific and Industrial Research
DSO	Distinguished Service Order
DWP	Department of Work and Pensions
DZ	Drop zone – paratroopers
ECT	Explosive cutting tape
FAPLA	Popular Front for the Liberation of Angola

FSB	Fire support base
GPMG	General Purpose Machine Gun
GR	Grid reference
GSG 9	Grenzschutzgruppe 9
HE	High-explosive
HMC	Ho Chi Minh City (formerly Saigon)
HQ	Headquarters
IED	Improvised explosive device
IRA	Irish Republican Army
IVCP	Illegal vehicle checkpoint
jebel	Mountain (Arabic)
JWS	Jungle Warfare School – Kota Tinggi, Johore Bahru, Malaysia
KFB	Loud explosion (Ker… fucking… boom!)
Khareef	Arabian monsoon
kraal	African village
LCT	Land clearing team
LO	Liaison officer
LZ	Landing zone – helicopter
MAG	7.62mm Machine Gun
MC	Military Cross
MiD	Mention in Dispatches
MP	Military police
MPLA	Popular Movement for the Liberation of Angola
NATO	North Atlantic Treaty Organisation
NCO	Non-commissioned officer

NI	Northern Ireland
NITAT	Northern Ireland Training and Advisory Team
NSTU	National Service Training Unit
NVA	North Vietnamese Army
OC	Officer commanding
OCS	Officer Cadet School
OP	Observation post
OR	other ranks (i.e. not commissioned)
Parabat	South African Parachute Battalion or paratrooper
PF	Permanent force
PJI	Parachute jump instructor
PMC	Private military company
PoW	Prisoner of war
PT	Physical training
R4	SADF 5.56mm assault rifle
RAAF	Royal Australian Air Force
RAASC	Royal Australian Army Service Corps
RAC	Royal Army Corps
RAPC	Royal Army Pay Corps
RAS	Reliance Aviation Security
RIB	Rigid inflatable boat
RMO	Regimental medical officer
RNZAF	Royal New Zealand Air Force
RO	Royal Ordnance
rondavel	Thatched hut (South Africa)
RP	Regimental policeman

RPG	Rocket-propelled grenade
RSM	Regimental sergeant major
RUC	Royal Ulster Constabulary
RV	Rendezvous
SAAF	South African Air Force
SADF	South African Defence Force
SAF	Sultan's Armed Forces (Oman)
SAS	Special Air Service
SBS	Special Boat Service
SDU	Special Duties Unit (Royal Hong Kong police maritime unit)
shona	Riverbed (South Africa)
SID	Seismic intruder detector
SIS	Secret Intelligence Services
SLR	Self-loading rifle
SNCO	Senior non-commissioned officer
SOAF	Sultan of Oman's Air Force
SOF	Special operations forces
SOP	Standard Operating Procedures
souk	Market (Sudan)
spoor	Enemy tracks (South Africa)
SSF	Sultan of Oman's Special Force
SWAPO	South West Africa People's Organisation
TA	Territorial Army
Toms	Parachute Regiment soldiers
UDR	Ulster Defence Regiment
UE	University entrance examination (New Zealand)

UN   United Nations

UNITA   National Union for the Total Independence of Angola (a pro-Western organisation formed in 1966 by Jonas Savimbi)

USMC   US Marine Corps

VC   Viet Cong

veldt   Open plains of South Africa (Afrikaans)

wadi   Valley/re-entrant (Arabic)

1

EARLY DAYS, 1948-65

I come from a proud line of soldiers. My father, Archibald McLea MacKenzie, was born in 1917. As early as he could, my father left home and joined the army as a Royal Artillery boy soldier. He enlisted in Stirling Castle where his grandfather had served in the Seaforth Highlanders. He was promoted to warrant officer in December 1939 at just 20 years old and was apparently the youngest warrant officer in the British Army. When he was courting my mother, he was arrested by a policeman on Brighton Esplanade. The bobby had ridden past on his bicycle, then rode back, jumped off his bike and arrested my father for impersonating a warrant officer. He just looked so young! He went to France with the British Expeditionary Force (BEF) and the 115th Regiment, Royal Artillery and was eventually evacuated from Dunkirk.

After returning from Dunkirk, my father trained with the 11th Armoured Division in England before returning to France in early June 1944 with the 75th Anti-tank Regiment, Royal Artillery as a troop commander of 17-pounder Achilles Sherman tank destroyers. He had a successful war, received a commission and was awarded three Mentions in Dispatches (MiD) – two on consecutive days. He did not receive a Military Cross (MC), to his eternal chagrin. His commanding officer (CO) at the time recognised that he deserved an MC but said he was, instead, recommending another officer who was a 'regular' and not a wartime commission like my father. The politics of bravery, no less!

My father remained in the army post-war. I was born in 1948 and as a family we moved around on multiple postings including Egypt and Cyprus. Eventually my father began work in the Claims Commission for the Ministry of Defence and for a while we settled down to a more ordinary family life in Bushey Heath, in south-east England. But soon a more exotic calling came along, and we were posted to Singapore where my father worked for Headquarters Far East Land Forces. The war had ended only ten years previously so memories of the brutal conflict in the Far East and actual physical reminders were everywhere. Just across the road from our house, near Pasir Panjang, were trenches where the Malay Regiment had put up a spirited defence against the Japanese in 1942. The men of C Company, 1st Battalion, the Malay Regiment, led by Lieutenant Adnan Bin Saidi, fought bravely to the last. Scores of Japanese soldiers were killed or wounded. But, vastly outnumbered, the Malay Regiment was eventually surrounded and massacred. Lieutenant Adnan Bin Saidi himself was tied in a sack, hung from a tree, and used for bayonet practice.

One day when some friends and I were playing in the old wartime trenches near our house I found a rusty 36 Mills hand grenade. We played with it for a while until someone called the Royal Engineers. Frightened that I would get into trouble, I threw it away. Unsurprisingly it caused a bit of a stink because they couldn't find it again.

My father was a very successful pugilist both when he was in the ranks and then later as an officer and won a number of trophies. I remember as a teenager challenging him, as boys do – I only ever did that once! He moved so quickly that I never knew where the slaps came from.

It had been an exotic childhood, living in four vastly different countries in just 11 years. But change was soon afoot once again. In 1959 my father decided to retire to New Zealand. He had received a job offer with the New Zealand Insurance Company. He was able, through his military connections, to obtain passage for us on the SS *Captain Cook*, which was returning to New Zealand with the 2nd New Zealand Regiment after a two-year tour in Malaya.

My sister Fiona, then aged 17, was the only eligible young lady on the boat, so was soon chatted up by all the young subalterns, especially one who later became a lieutenant general – they might have become an item had my parents not disapproved because he was Catholic. Others on the boat, such as Brian Monks and Danny Waratini, would feature in my later New Zealand Army life.

As we were leaving Singapore we were anchored beside the fuel bunkers on Pulau Bukum, refuelling, and I recall watching with horrid fascination as huge sharks began eating the debris beside the ship. They would swim up to the food, turn on their backs, a huge mouth filled with razor-sharp teeth would open, the food would be gobbled up and then they would gracefully roll over to dive down again and swim away. We sailed to New Zealand via Freemantle, Perth, where I watched as late arrivals from the battalion overnight shore leave were trying to climb up the mooring lines as we were preparing to depart.

Finally, on a grey, wet and miserable day in December 1959 we entered Lyttelton Harbour in the South Island of New Zealand. My mother looked in horror at the little wooden houses clustered together on the damp hillside. Remarkably, my future wife Cecilia's father, who was in the Department of Agriculture, came out with the other officials to greet the boat as it arrived in Lyttelton. It is, indeed, a small world.

We disembarked and went by bus to a reception for the battalion at King Edward Barracks in Christchurch, before re-boarding the ship that night for Wellington. After disembarking we left the tender mercies of the New Zealand Army and spent a couple of nights in a hotel at the top of Willis Street. Even today I clearly remember the all-pervading smell of stale beer in the corridors. Wellington was not the cosmopolitan city then that it is now. Hotels were very basic and, as in the rest of New Zealand at that time, alcohol could not be served after 6pm, leading to the infamous 'six o'clock swill'. We initially settled in York's Bay, where I made friends with our neighbours the Atkinsons, a long-standing York Bay family. I had several trips on the beautiful wooden vessel *St Michael*, built by the inimitable Tudor Atkinson DSC, the family patriarch. I remember being extremely sea-sick coming back from Palliser Bay after one trip, much to the amusement of the nautical Atkinson family.

I attended Wellesley College in nearby Days Bay: a tough, no-nonsense, all-boys school where the leather strap was used freely on the hand. I had a Singapore wicker school basket that my mother insisted I used as my New Zealand school bag. I was very embarrassed to have to carry this on the school bus each day and my new Kiwi school 'friends' ridiculed me mercilessly. But with the sea at the end of the road for fishing, swimming and snorkelling, life was still good.

Finally we settled permanently in Wellington itself, and I attended secondary school at the prestigious Wellington College. The school had a grand, capacious assembly hall with a beautiful stained-glass window of St George fighting the dragon. In front of this window, on a raised platform, sat the various teachers, resplendent in their robes and mortar boards. The walls were covered with varnished boards remembering the many College old boys who had died on active service in both world wars.

Our Latin teacher was 'Inky' Deighton. Inky always wore his master's cape and controlled his classes with a rod of iron. He had served in World War I as a sniper and we always tried hard to get him to recount some war stories. Occasionally he would oblige. A great favourite was the one of him and a German sniper locked in a deadly duel. They had been stalking each other for some days trying to identify each other's shooting positions. With great drama Inky would state, 'The first one to move died ... he moved!'

I did not excel at academics but I was heavily involved in the school cadet corps, and spent several weeks each year at cadet camps in Linton Army Camp during the long summer holidays. I became the school's senior under-officer. I vividly remember being on the rifle range during cadet camp one year and watching a number of Bren guns being fired together at the targets. I could only imagine the horror of having to attack into automatic fire like that.

I also belonged to the Tararua Tramping Club, which I joined when I was around 14 years old. I used to go to their meetings on a Tuesday evening in their clubrooms near the Basin Reserve and then go on tramps in the Tararuas in the weekends. The Tararua Mountains are north of Wellington and are a great bush-clad area with steep mountains, their tops covered in tarns amongst the tussock and alpine plants. We would set off from Wellington on a Friday night and do a night tramp to a hut and then do a circuit before returning to Wellington on a Sunday afternoon. It was hard work walking up riverbeds in the dark but worth it once you got into the bush proper. The tramping club huts were very basic with chicken-wire bunks and not much else. Some of the 'long-drops' though had the most amazing views over the surrounding bush-covered hills. This is where I developed my love for the outdoors and living in the bush.

I was seemingly destined for a career in the armed forces but at the time I actually wanted to be a veterinary surgeon or go into the forestry service. But academics continued to elude me. In 1964 I managed to scrape a pass in my school certificate exam and progressed to the Sixth Form to study for the University Entrance (UE) exam. I had done well in school cadets and in 1965 I attended the regular officer selection board in Waiouru. I passed the board and was accepted for the Officer Cadet School in Portsea, Australia, on the condition I passed my UE.

The UE was normally accredited based on the full year's class work and exams. One Friday some friends and I 'wagged' school to camp outside Athletic Park to get tickets to watch the All Blacks play France the next day. Unfortunately, we were seen on television by the school headmaster who immediately refused to credit us with any coursework, so that we would have to rely solely on passing the end-of-year exams. I sat a few of the exams but my marks were appallingly low and I had no chance of passing. Eventually I changed my core subjects, replacing Latin, chemistry and maths with geography, biology and bookkeeping. I passed the following year. A military future now beckoned.

2

NEW ZEALAND ARMY, 1966-73

In December 1965, the New Zealand Army contacted me to see if I had passed the University Entrance exam and if I was still interested in a career in the armed forces. I formally enlisted in the army on 9 February 1966 in Army Headquarters in Wellington. I made friends with Ian Glendenning because we travelled to Waiouru on the train to start our basic training course together. He was from Christchurch and was also an officer cadet. I was his best man in 1969, and we went to Singapore and then Vietnam together. Sadly he shot himself in 1980. On reaching Waiouru I commenced 12 months' training as an infantry private soldier before I would be able to attend Officer Cadet School (OCS) in Portsea, Australia. The infantry training involved a ten-week basic soldiering course in the Army Recruit Depot in Waiouru in the centre of the North Island, followed by infantry corps training in Burnham in the middle of the South Island near Christchurch; and then an instructors' course in Waiouru and Fiji, as well as the normal basic training. It was hard work but as a potential officer you saw the other side of soldiering and it was excellent preparation before being commissioned.

Basic soldiering was tough but enjoyable and, having been a school cadet, I had lived in similar conditions before. Stand-out memories of Basic Course are of the battle fitness tests – 10-mile runs in ill-fitting, uncomfortable fatigues held up by a safety pin which kept undoing; of hours spent on the rifle ranges; of getting 14 days confined to barracks (CB) from the Training Depot Commanding Officer for under-age drinking at the Waiouru Tavern after getting busted by the military police walking back to camp; and of chasing the Orderly Room bugle at 6am until 9pm as part of the CB punishment. When undergoing CB you were at the mercy of the orderly sergeant outside normal working hours or over the whole of a weekend. Whenever the regular bugle calls sounded we had to race to the orderly sergeant's hut in the unit HQ dressed in whatever uniform he had previously ordered. He could also order us to report at any other time. At the weekends as well as 'chasing the bugle', as we called it, we would have to do fatigues around the camp such as 'peeling spuds' in the various cookhouses or cleaning pots and pans. CB was no fun! An 18-year-old soldier could go to war but was deemed too young to drink or vote.

After basic training in Waiouru, together with my fellow infantry colleagues, I was posted to the 1st Battalion, Royal New Zealand Infantry Regiment (1 RNZIR) Depot in Burnham. We moved into a World War II-era long, cold barrack room with a useless pot-belly stove in the middle. We carried out our infantry corps training here, and at the end of our training we were awarded the coveted Red Diamond to be worn on our uniform showing we were fully trained infantrymen.

The 1st Battalion, RNZIR had been formed on 1 May 1964. It was the result of a post-war decision to abolish ten separate infantry regiments, which together had formed the Royal New Zealand Infantry Corps, and instead form a single infantry regiment with numbered battalions. At the time I joined up there were two active regular infantry battalions: the 1st and 2nd Battalions. The unit insignia of the 2nd Battalion was retained and worn on the upper left sleeve of battalion members. This red diamond was awarded to soldiers after they successfully completed their infantry corps training, and now I was finally one of them.

After receiving our red diamonds we were then permitted to move into the main barracks with the 'real' soldiers. We lived with a number of veterans who had served in Borneo during the

Indonesian Confrontation (1962–66). Shortly after moving into these newer barracks I bought a sleeping bag from another soldier for £5. I was very happy with my new purchase which meant I did not have to use the issue blankets when we were in the field. But I was then horrified to find out that the sleeping bag had in fact been stolen from a giant of a Maori Borneo veteran called 'Buck' Piper. I promptly hid the sleeping bag and never used again it for the entire time I was in the army.

We did our field training in a place called Little Malaya in the foothills of the Southern Alps where the bush was always very cold and wet. We carried extremely heavy, old World War II canvas webbing and packs. We went on long runs around the Burnham area along the straight endless dirt roads of the Canterbury Plains. We also spent a lot of time in the Tekapo training area which was on the edge of the Southern Alps and generally under several feet of snow in winter. Constant training and drilling in these inhospitable conditions toughened us up considerably.

One Friday night on weekend leave I was in Christchurch with Ian Glendenning, the friend I had made when we first signed up. We bumped into an older fellow soldier called Kelly Tamarapa. To Ian's total surprise he saw that Kelly was wearing his suit and must have broken into his wardrobe to get it. When Ian asked him what the hell he was doing he said, 'You were in town and you can't wear two suits at once, bro!' This clear logic left Ian speechless.

In early 1967 I was posted to OCS Portsea for 12 months. There, I knew most of the other Kiwi cadets from basic training in New Zealand. I was to meet many of my Portsea colleagues when I was later serving in Vietnam. It was a hard 12 months. We spent six months as the junior class and six months as the senior class. There was a system of 'fathers' and 'sons' to assist the classes to settle in, that is, new cadets had 'fathers' from the senior class and then became 'fathers' in their own senior class. My 'son' was an Australian called Trevor Bayo whom I later met in Vietnam and we subsequently laughed together over some of the weird things we had endured at OCS. We trained hard and studied hard, interrupted by field exercises, drill, tough physical training (PT), and rugby.

There was a stone memorial near the parade ground and classrooms at OCS with the names of OCS officers who had been killed in action. When I arrived at Portsea there were just two names and when I left there were about eight. Passing this memorial each day tended to focus the mind on what this was all about.

Despite the intense pressure we all worked well together. The cadet school was located at the end of the Nepean peninsula in Melbourne. It was in a popular recreational area and in summer scores of bikini-clad women would take pleasure in water-skiing past the water-front parade ground. Woe betide any cadet who allowed his eyes to follow the water-skiers during drill movements. The other main hazard was horse flies. These monster flies would land ever so gently on exposed skin, normally a face or neck, walk about a bit, and then give you the most painful bite. It was a real test of self-discipline – you knew the bite was coming but you could do nothing about it!

The Australian bush where we carried out field exercises was totally different to what us Kiwis were used to. New Zealand wildlife is relatively benign while nearly all the creatures in the Australian bush seemed to want to kill you! We soon learned all about these 'nasties'. The Australian cadets gleefully 'helped' our knowledge with colourful stories of 'drop-bears' and 'hoop snakes'. The former were apparently vicious little bears that would drop on the head of any unsuspecting traveller in the bush and the latter were supposedly poisonous snakes that would wait on the top of a hill until an unsuspecting Kiwi came along and they would then put their tails in their mouths and rapidly roll down the slopes of the hill to attack their prey. We were all too ready to believe them!

At Portsea, Kiwis were, for all intents and purposes, Australian soldiers and we wore their uniforms and equipment and carried their weapons. I still proudly have my Australian infantry slouch hat, although somewhere in my travels a puppy has chewed some bits out of the brim. There was always good-natured rivalry between these two nationalities at Portsea and we also had cadets from Malaysia and Papua New Guinea thrown into the mix.

I had to work hard, for as always as I was not a natural student. I graduated successfully in the top third of the class and my parents came over from New Zealand for the graduation parade and ceremony. It was nice for them to see me graduate and I hope I made them proud.

After Christmas leave in New Zealand I was posted as a second lieutenant with the Portsea graduates to Waiouru Camp on the young officers course. We linked up with other graduates from Australia's Duntroon and the United Kingdom's Sandhurst military academies. We Portsea graduates proudly considered ourselves as the army's cannon fodder. The young officers course was hectic; I met some great officers and we thoroughly enjoyed mess life. At the end of the course I was posted as a platoon commander to a National Service Training Unit (NSTU) still in Waiouru. I was now in command of a platoon of national servicemen but I was taught quite a few things by some older senior non-commissioned officers (SNCO). One of them, Danny Waratini, had been on the SS *Captain Cook* in 1959 with us. One of my assistant officer cadets was a Fijian called Sitiveni 'Steve' Rambuka, who later carried out a military coup in Fiji and eventually became the prime minister. He was a powerful man and an excellent soldier. He and I have remained good friends.

Commanding the NSTU was a good learning environment and afterwards I was posted back to the 1st Battalion Depot in Burnham as a platoon commander under Major Laurie P, the company commander. He was due to take us to Vietnam. He was a bluff, congenial officer and we all enjoyed working with him. In mid-1968 I met my future wife, Cecilia, at an officers' mess party in Christchurch. In February 1969 I went to Fiji on jungle training and, on our return, I had to admit to Cecilia that I was actually only 21, not 23. I had been hoping to impress her with my maturity! Luckily, she still agreed to marry me.

Meanwhile I continued to improve and hone my military skills. In mid-1969, I completed a basic parachute course at the Royal New Zealand Air Force (RNZAF) Parachute Training and Support Unit (PTSU) at Whenuapai airbase near Auckland. Places on this course were hard to come by. It was a tough course run by Captain Albie Kiwi of the New Zealand Special Air Service (SAS). He was a hard man and for charity had once run the length of New Zealand with his dog 'Sass' who had to wear small custom-made leather booties on his paws. Albie did not exactly take a shine to me and made my life rather difficult. Tragically, Albie would be killed in a parachuting accident while subsequently serving with the Australian Army.

Certainly, the SAS personnel who ran the course alongside the RNZAF made sure there was a high element of PT and endurance. It was a great course, although somewhat scary, and so started my love-hate relationship with the air which continues to this day.

We parachuted from the C-47 Douglas 'Dakota' which we called the Para-Dak. The Dakota had, of course, seen extensive service during World War II delivering airborne troops across Europe. When I later joined the British Parachute Regiment I was proud to be able able to say that I had trained to parachute from a Dakota. The Dakota had been long gone from UK parachute training and the only reminder of this great World War II Para workhorse was the static display aircraft located outside the Depot of the Parachute Regiment and Airborne Forces in Aldershot.

The course involved a total of eight descents. We had to complete two descents by day and two by night in 'clean fatigue' which meant with no equipment and another two by day and two by night with equipment. Our equipment consisted of our large pack or bergen wrapped up in a container which was clipped to our waists and then lowered to the end of a suspension rope once we were hanging beneath our parachute. This equipment hit the ground before the owner and at least gave a bit of warning at night of how soon you were going land. Prior to our first parachute descent we were taken on a training flight in which we carried out all the procedures for parachuting but did not actually jump out of the aircraft. This practice flight was often undertaken in windy weather which would not have been suitable for actual parachuting. Each potential paratrooper had to stand in the open door of the aircraft with his face in the slipstream – this was certainly an experience when the aircraft was in turbulent air.

On one of my early NZ para drops I was descending towards some sheep which had wandered onto the grassy drop zone (DZ). If I had landed on one, we would both have been badly hurt so I started shouting at them. Of course, they had no idea where I was and started running around in circles directly below me. Luckily, I missed them all!

Cecilia and I were married in the small iconic stone Church of the Good Shepherd on 18 October 1969 on the shores of Lake Tekapo: a place I had passed many times on my way to and from Tekapo training camp. I was promoted to lieutenant; moreover, I had been formally posted to 1 RNZIR in Singapore and we arrived in December of that same year.

SERVICE IN SINGAPORE

We had a house outside of military quarters and it was fascinating to be back amongst the sights, sounds and smells of the Far East. My first introduction to overseas military life was being made duty officer for the battalion over the Christmas period of 1969–70. Unsurprisingly, all the 'new' officers had some sort of duty over this period.

Straight after the Christmas leave had finished we spent most of the following weeks in the jungles of Malaya with our platoons carrying out pre-Vietnam training. A number of our instructors had never served in Vietnam and it puzzled me that with the high numbers of Vietnam veterans in the battalion we were being taught by NCOs whose experience of jungle fighting was against the communist insurgents or the Indonesians in Borneo – both types of opposition were quite different to the foe we were expecting to face in South Vietnam.

During one pre-Vietnam training exercise in Malaya we were carrying out a typical night-time platoon patrol through a rubber plantation. I was in the centre of the formation. Suddenly the ground gave way beneath me and I started falling into a hole.

Luckily, I had my self-loading rifle (SLR) across my chest and that combined with my elbows stopped me plummeting into the depths below. I was helped out of the hole by one of my NCOs. I got out my torch and peered into the hole. It was a smooth cylindrical hole about 15–20 feet deep and writhing and coiling at the bottom there must have been about 20 snakes of various varieties. It would have been a painful and unpleasant demise if I had fallen to the bottom! I suspect it had once been a well for the plantation, but had since dried up. I had more than a few sleepless nights reliving the event!

As the weeks passed my platoon became a well-trained, well-honed infantry group, comfortable with each other and ready for our imminent deployment to Vietnam. I used to receive regular letters from a fellow OCS officer, Bill Blair, who was already on a tour of duty in Vietnam. His letters were a goldmine of useful information, particularly highlighting operational mistakes, and I always shared all relevant information with my platoon.

A month or so before I deployed to Vietnam we moved to new housing in the former British Army base in Nee Soon Garrison. The housing area itself had some amusing British Army idiosyncrasies – it backed onto some thick jungle and behind the houses where the captains and majors lived there was quite a substantial wire fence. However, as the fence passed behind the first of the subalterns' houses it shrank into a two-strand garden fence. The local monkeys would come out of the jungle, jump over this little fence and stick their arms through the window netting of the kitchen to try to steal food. They could be very aggressive if they decided to visit in a big mob. Slightly more scary was the occasional visit from a python. Our pet cat unfortunately ended up being a tasty snack for one such caller!

OPERATIONAL SERVICE IN SOUTH VIETNAM 1970-71

In 1970 New Zealand had a population of just 2.5 million and a small professional army consisting of one regular brigade and three Territorial Army brigades. Throughout the conflict in

Vietnam, New Zealand provided a small but effective military contribution and this military contribution was, in fact, almost one third of the entire regular army. It all began with a small contingent of engineers who arrived in theatre in June 1964 to perform a non-combat role of bridge and road-building. This small unit was followed in mid-July 1965 by 161 Battery of the Royal New Zealand Artillery, the only regular artillery unit in the New Zealand Army, who deployed in support of the US 173rd Airborne Brigade, the first time Kiwi forces were deployed in a combat role in Vietnam. The first infantry unit, a reinforced company group from the 1st Battalion, arrived in Vietnam in March 1967, with a second company following in December of that year. The two initial company groups, supported by mortars and assault pioneers, were designated Victor and Whisky companies, names that would stick for the duration of the war as companies were rotated in and out of theatre. The New Zealand troops would be attached to the 1st Australian Task Force based at Nui Dat, approximately 60 miles from Saigon City, in the Phuoc Tuy Province, continuing the proud Australian and New Zealand Army Corps (ANZAC) tradition first begun in World War I.

The early contingents to Vietnam only stayed for six months but the majority of subsequent tours were for 365 days. The Kiwi infantry soldiers were based in Malaya or, later, Singapore prior to going to Vietnam and so they were accustomed to operating in the jungle. The Kiwi way of operating was by stealth and guile and by the time that the unit was posted to Vietnam it had worked together for a long time. Each member of the unit knew his job and could operate well as part of the team. The Kiwi infantry rightly earned themselves a reputation as formidable jungle fighters.

Once a New Zealand rifle company had completed its tour it would be replaced by another complete company and this system ensured that the unit *esprit de corps* was maintained. In contrast the American forces in Vietnam had a trickle reinforcement system and this made the establishment of any unit *esprit de corps* difficult with FNGs (fucking new guys) regularly arriving.

Each man in the eight- to ten-man section of a platoon was a specialist in one particular area. He was a rifleman, a machine gunner, a grenadier or a lead scout. But each man was also cross-trained for the other jobs in the patrol. Lead scouts were selected for their tracking ability and keen observation and were trained to an extremely high level of expertise. They were the eyes and ears of the patrol and so they had to be the best. Movement through the jungle, affectionately called the 'J', was slow and garden secateurs were used to snip through the undergrowth enabling patrols to move soundlessly. Garden saws were sometimes used in extremely heavy bush, while the use of the machete was restricted to emergencies only, such as creating an emergency landing zone (LZ).

The primary weapon of the New Zealand infantry soldier was the 7.62mm self-loading (SLR) FN rifle, nicknamed the 'elephant gun' by our American compatriots, who were used to the much lighter M16 rifle. We preferred our SLR because when we hit the enemy, he stayed down! The section automatic weapon was the US M60 machine gun. Normally we would have used the British-manufactured general purpose machine gun (GPMG). But the manufacturers had informed the New Zealand Army that if Kiwi troops used the GPMG in Vietnam then they would no longer sell the gun to us. Similarly, the manufacturers of the section anti-tank weapon used by the New Zealand Army, the 84mm Carl Gustav, also refused to allow the weapons to be used in Vietnam by using threats of stopping future supplies of spare parts or replacements. I doubt anyone in the infantry complained about that, however, as it is a heavy 'dog' of a weapon to carry.

Lead scouts had a choice between the SLR, which was only semi-automatic, the M16 or the M203. The M203 was an M16 rifle with an M79 grenade launcher beneath the rifle barrel. This grenade launcher had a variety of ammunition that could be used with it. The most commonly available types were the high-explosive (HE) round, the buckshot round and the very effective illumination round. If a scout carried an M203, it would generally be loaded with an HE grenade because the buckshot round was not considered particularly effective. Lead scouts preferred taking their chances with some shrapnel splashback from the HE grenade rather than allowing a Viet Cong (VC) to get away. But unquestionably the favourite weapon was the claymore directional mine containing a pound of HE and 700 ball bearings. The Kiwi infantrymen thought the claymore was 'better than canned beer' – a high accolade indeed from hard-drinking colonial men.

The weather in Vietnam was hot and horrible in the dry season (November to April) and worse in the wet season (May to October). Average temperatures were in the mid-30 degrees Celsius by day and only dropped to the mid-20s at night, combined with 100 per cent humidity during the wet season. In the wet season, as regular as clockwork, at 3pm, the monsoon rains would arrive in great downpours. If we were still patrolling it was too early to set up a night ambush position so we were soaked to the skin for the entire length of the operation. The normal trick of keeping a dry set of clothes in your pack for sleeping was a pointless exercise because you had immediately to man the perimeter in the event of enemy action or conduct sentry duty at night – all in the rain. The only good point of the wet season was the availability of water. In the dry season there was no water and we could only drink what we carried until resupplied after a number of days. Heat exhaustion in the dry season was a constant possibility for the heavily laden infantryman. We carried numerous water bottles with us as well as a water bag which could be rolled up when empty. Our water bags were plastic and not very robust, so we usually tried to cadge the American types which were both bigger and better. The American lightweight camouflage poncho-liners also became prized items amongst us Kiwi troops.

Operations would generally be for three weeks at a time either from the main base at Nui Dat or from firebases situated further out in the province. Each night, ambushes would be placed using a triangle formation which experience had shown was the best method of using the combined effect of the claymore, M60s and artillery support fire. Each soldier in the platoon, excluding the machine gunners and radio operators, would carry at least one claymore mine and 2 or 3 feet of detonating cord. The detonating cord enabled the claymore mines to be laid in groups along an ambush site. Claymores were sighted to fire down tracks not across them as that tended to blow the enemy into the jungle on the far side of the track out of the killing zone.

On each patrol the troops would start out with a minimum of five days' food and water plus ammunition, claymores, spare belts of ammunition for the M60, C4 explosives and spare radio batteries. This enabled each group to be totally independent for as long as possible. Occasionally operations would be extended up to 10–14 days, but this was only in extreme cases. Long-range patrols were the task of the New Zealand and Australian SAS patrols also based at Nui Dat. The main task of the Kiwi infantry was search and destroy missions. Intelligence would be received that the local Viet Cong (the only regular North Vietnamese Army (NVA) unit in Phuoc Tuy was a small but lethal engineer unit) were operating in a particular area, and the ANZAC forces would be deployed against them. Phuoc Tuy was one of the traditional infiltration routes into Saigon and so there was always 'work to be had'. The normal method of deployment from Nui Dat into the field was by helicopter from the Royal Australian Air Force (RAAF) based in Vung Tau. Sometimes M113 APCs (armoured personnel carriers) would be used to move into the operational zone but they were highly vulnerable to mines and were noisy in the jungle. Troops rode on the top of the APCs to make maximum use of the 'baffle' provided by the hull of the vehicle in the event of it hitting a mine. The troops were more vulnerable to small arms fire when on the top of the armoured vehicle, but they feared mine explosions far more so considered it worth the risk.

Initially in a deployment a fire support base (FSB) would be established with artillery pieces flown in as necessary. From the firebases companies were deployed and established mortar firebases and from these bases half-platoon patrols would operate around the base looking for the enemy. A very large area could be covered by numerous patrols extending fanlike out from the centre.

Patrols would move in single file through the jungle. Moving first would be the pair of scouts travelling a tactical bound ahead of the rest of patrol. The lead scout would always be covered by the cover scout. Behind them would be either the M60 team or the patrol commander depending on whether contact was imminent or not.

The patrol commander would have a pace-counter taped to the pistol grip of his weapon. This little device is used in the Antipodes for counting sheep but in Vietnam it was used for counting paces. This, used in conjunction with the metal military prismatic compass, assisted the commander in navigating in the jungle with its complete absence of landmarks. Standard plastic compasses were no good as they were simply melted by the vicious insect repellent we were forced to use. Of course, accurate navigation also meant that when we called for artillery fire it didn't land on our heads!

After the patrol commander would come the signaller, then the grenadier and then a rifle group with a 'tail-end Charlie' covering the back of the patrol. If the enemy was sighted and there was not enough time to establish a quick ambush, the scouts would initiate the firefight and go to either side of their route. The M60 'hot sauce machine' would then move to a fire position left or right and pour in the fire. A rifle group would go to the opposite side to the M60 and in this way a firebase was rapidly established and the task of winning the firefight immediately started.

If the patrol was platoon or company size than the remainder of the platoon would form the left and right side of the triangle with the base already formed by the patrol in contact. This meant that if Viet Cong tried to roll up the position from a flank they would find another baseline waiting for them. Other platoons on the move would also form into a triangle with M60s on each point ready to fire across the front of each of the baselines with defilade fire.

The Kiwi is a natural soldier. Those of Polynesian stock are normally of great physique and strength. It was extremely common in Vietnam to see huge, grinning Maoris with layers of belted bullets slung around their shoulders. But Kiwis are not formal soldiers and this stems from their colonial outdoor heritage. Officers in theatre have to earn the respect of their soldiers and this is not given as a matter of course to go with the rank. This mutual respect between officers and enlisted men plus the fact that the New Zealand Armed Forces are very small means that each unit becomes very close-knit and effective. Vietnam was no exception to this. The kill ratio for most Victor and Whisky companies was always at least 10:1.

As in more recent conflicts the Kiwi units had a very small logistic 'tail'. In Vietnam they were being supported by the Australian Task Force. There were not too many REMFs (Rear Echelon Mother-fuckers); almost all the Kiwis in Vietnam were out 'humping the boonies' looking for 'Charlie'. I was about to become one of them.

I left for Vietnam on 8 May 1970 as the platoon commander of 3 Platoon, Victor 5 Company: an appointment I held for the full 12 months of our operational tour. We landed at the 1st Australian Task Force (1 ATF) logistic base at Vung Tau. Here we were issued with live ammunition and grenades and loaded on to Australian trucks for the one-hour journey north along Highway 15 and then Route 2 to our destination. We were to be attached to the 2nd Royal Australian Regiment (2 RAR), part of the Australian Task Force located in a major firebase in Nui Dat. We sat on the trucks with our loaded rifles looking outwards with a certain amount of trepidation but a great deal of interest. We passed through small villages clustered on the sides of the road. We drove past mopeds by the score and, less frequently, bullock carts. Most of the villagers were wearing the distinctive bamboo conical hat that continues to typify Vietnam. Bridges were guarded by small Vietnamese Army soldiers wearing tight-fitting camouflage uniforms inside concrete bunkers. Many of the bunkers and bridges showed signs of damage from small arms fire. As we left the area of Vung Tau the countryside opened up and we could see the Nui Thi Vai and Nui Toc Thien Mountains to the north-west. These were nicknamed the 'Wolvertons' after a popular song of the time. We could also just see through the haze the dreaded Long Hai Mountains to the east. The Long Hai Mountains had by this point already caused many mine casualties to the Australians operating in them. I would have my own share of mine casualties in the Wolvertons; however, this was still to come.

We drove through the badly damaged town of Baria, which had been the scene of fierce fighting during the Tet Offensive of 1968. The Viet Cong had been finally surrounded in the town's movie theatre and the building had been all but destroyed. Looking at these shattered buildings gave us a dramatic insight into the war so far.

I had been with my platoon for a full 18 months by this point so we knew each other well. Our officer commanding was now Major John Mc, a Duntroon graduate. My platoon sergeant was Dave 'Pancho' Beattie, an experienced senior non-commissioned officer (SNCO).

I took over from Lieutenant Stan Kidd of Victor 4 Company. He had been killed in action while looking for a wounded Viet Cong after a contact. When I arrived to take over his tent it only had a low line of sandbags surrounding it. I think a number of sandbags had been 'liberated' after the previous owner was killed. It took some prompting to get my platoon sergeant to organise the filling of extra sandbags to raise the level to the height of all the other tents. Such was the introduction to my 12-month tour.

As Victor 5 Company we completed the ANZAC Battalion consisting of the three Australian rifle companies (A, B and C) of the 2nd Royal Australian Regiment (2 RAR) and the New Zealand Whisky 3 Company who were halfway through their tour when we arrived in theatre. The Support Company was augmented by two New Zealand mortar sections, two pioneer sections, and a Kiwi major as second-in-command of the battalion. The New Zealand soldiers were all volunteers whereas almost half of the Australian

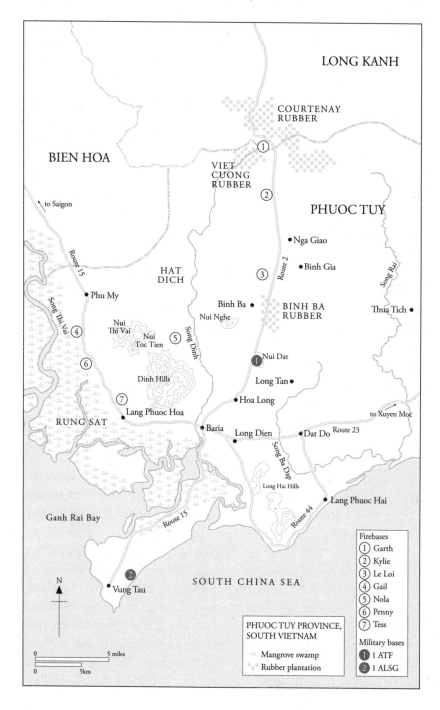

LONG KANH

COURTENAY
RUBBER

BIEN HOA

VIET
CUONG
RUBBER

to Saigon

PHUOC TUY

Route 15

• Nga Giao

• Binh Gia

HAT
DICH

Route 2

Song Rai

• Phu My

Binh Ba •

Nui Nghe

BINH BA
RUBBER

Thua Tich •

Song Thi Vai

Nui
Thi Vai

Nui
Toc Tien

Song Dinh

Nui Dat

Dinh Hills

Long Tan •

• Hoa Long

to Xuyen Moc

Lang Phuoc Hoa

RUNG SAT

• Baria

Long Dien

• Dat Do

Route 23

Song Ba Dap

Long Hai Hills

Route 44

• Lang Phuoc Hai

Ganh Rai Bay

Route 15

N

• Vung Tau

SOUTH CHINA SEA

Firebases
① Garth
② Kylie
③ Le Loi
④ Gail
⑤ Nola
⑥ Penny
⑦ Tess

Military bases
❶ 1 ATF
❷ 1 ALSG

PHUOC TUY PROVINCE,
SOUTH VIETNAM

Mangrove swamp
Rubber plantation

0   5 miles

0   5km

soldiers were conscripts and had not volunteered for service in Vietnam.

A day after our arrival in Nui Dat we started some two weeks of 'in-country' training. This involved a great deal of shooting on the rifle range on the outskirts of the Task Force base as well as demonstrations of the weapons and equipment that would be available to support us, including APCs, tanks, artillery and fire support helicopters, which could be Huey gunships or the particularly awesome Cobra gunships. We also practised casualty evacuation drills with the medical evacuation (medevac) 'dust-off' choppers. The three platoon commanders went out on a number of heli recces over the battalion's area of operations (AO). The contrast between the open rice fields and the thick primary jungle was most obvious and the steep mountains of the Wolvertons looked especially forbidding. The Firestone Trails cut a swathe across the countryside on the west of our AO. These were massive cleared areas which had been carved out of the jungle by enormous armoured bulldozers called 'Rome ploughs'. These trails were 200–300 yards wide; they disrupted VC infiltration routes and allowed aerial observation of likely VC trails. They also permitted movement of armoured vehicles but were frequently mined and booby-trapped. Initially, each platoon went out on one- or two-day patrols around the perimeter of Nui Dat. These were 'shakedown patrols' and we used them to become familiar with the battalion's Standard Operating Procedures (SOP) as well as the numerous types of reports and messages that would need to be sent to our company HQ, from contact reports and mine incident reports to resupply requests. One of my first patrols was through the rubber plantation near the hamlet of Long Tan on the outskirts of Nui Dat. This plantation was the scene of fierce fighting between soldiers of D Company, 6 RAR and some 1,500 VC from D445 Battalion and 275th Regiment on 18–21 August 1966. The Australians lost 18 killed and the VC approximately 245 killed. The trees in the plantation were still shattered from the heavy artillery support fire from Nui Dat and my compass was unreliable due to the metal in the ground from the battle.

The ANZAC Battalion's extra rifle company was the envy of other Task Force infantry battalions until October 1970 when Whisky 3 Company left at the end of its tour and was not replaced. We in Victor 5 Company completed our tour in May 1971 and we were ultimately replaced by Victor 6 Company, which remained in Vietnam with 4 RAR to perpetuate the ANZAC Battalion for another seven months until the start of the phased withdrawal from Vietnam.

The Australian Task Force (1 ATF) committed to South Vietnam comprised the following combat and support arms: one armoured squadron equipped with Centurion main battle tanks; one armoured personnel carrier squadron equipped with M113 APCs; one field artillery regiment equipped with 105mm howitzers; one field engineer squadron; one engineer construction squadron; one signal squadron; three infantry battalions (including the five companies from the ANZAC Battalion); one SAS squadron (plus a troop of NZSAS); and one reconnaissance flight equipped with Sioux light observation helicopters and Porter fixed-wing aircraft. The Royal Australian Air Force provided transport including one helicopter squadron with UH1H 'Huey' helicopters and one short-range transport aircraft detachment equipped with Caribou transport aircraft.

We also had fire support available from the US consisting of one medium artillery company equipped with 155mm guns; one heavy artillery platoon equipped with 8-inch guns; and one anti-aircraft platoon equipped with twin 40mm 'dusters' for close protection of artillery fire units.

These dusters were based in Nui Dat and the US officer commanding the group had recently disciplined a number of his soldiers for using marijuana. The morning after, he awoke to find that there was a duster on its tracked chassis at each corner of his tent with the barrels pointing into the tent! This was certainly a variation from the threat of being 'fragged' by a grenade.

Working with armoured vehicles in close country was interesting, to say the least. We were familiar with the M113 APC, having worked with them in New Zealand, but we had not operated with the Australian 52-ton main battle tank, the Centurion, prior to this. Despite its large size at nearly 10 feet high, 11 feet wide and 32 feet long, it was very difficult in jungle conditions to pinpoint its exact location. Rendezvous (RV) procedures had to be well coordinated in close country and a decision made as to whether we would move to the tanks or they would come to us. If these procedures were not closely followed there was a good chance of us 'grunts' being squished by these monsters or blown to pieces. The first you knew where they were was when the long 20-pounder barrel parted the trees and bushes as it growled along towards you. These Australian Centurion tanks carried canister rounds as well as high-explosive shells. The canister rounds were giant shotgun shells that were ideal for clearing enemy bunker systems. They also carried .30-calibre and .50-calibre turret-mounted machine guns. A troop of four tanks could carry a platoon of infantry with a section on each vehicle and platoon HQ mounted on the troop commander's tank.

These tanks were remarkably good at moving through close country and secondary jungle but remaining on board without getting swept off by trees and branches or getting trapped by a rotating turret had to be learned very quickly. We mainly operated with the tanks when we were patrolling out of firebases along the Firestone Trails. In these situations, it was reassuring to have them with you or on the firebase perimeter with their formidable firepower.

On one patrol I was instructed to link up with a troop of tanks in thick jungle. I advised the OC (officer commanding) that we were OK and that they were too noisy for us. Nevertheless, the link-up was carried out, slowly and carefully. As I finally linked up with the Australian troop commander on his tank, who had obviously been listening on our company radio net, he looked down at me, a lowly, smelly infantryman, and said, with a slight sneer, in his broad Aussie accent, 'If we are too noisy for you, mate, we can always fuck off again.'

Along with the support provided to us by our own and the allocated US fire units, we could also call for gunfire support from any Australian or US naval vessel in range of the Vietnamese coast, or request sorties from US ground-attack aircraft.

The provision of good intelligence is important in any counter-insurgency warfare and the intelligence process played a significant role in all operations undertaken by the Task Force. There were various sources of information about the enemy in Phuoc Tuy but the degree of reliability of that information was widely variable. Information was obtained through physical, chemical and electronic means. Physical sources included our own unit reports, prisoners of war, surrendered enemy personnel and captured enemy documents. The main chemical means was the 'sniffer' aircraft. These aircraft carried devices for detecting the odours of humans and their habitation. The aircraft made low-level sweeps across suspected enemy areas. There were also several electronic devices for gaining early information of enemy movement. One was the acoustic and seismic intruder detector (SID). Aircraft dropped these detectors astride the likely enemy lines of approach. They emitted radio signals when started by either enemy sound or vibration. The Task Force intelligence unit maintained records of all reports of enemy activity and also kept a record of enemy activity in every map square in the province. This intelligence with the recent aerial photographs was available to units for study before every operation.

The province of Phuoc Tuy assumed a roughly rectangular shape, with the upper left-hand corner removed. It covered an area of about 725 square miles. Its length from west to east was approximately 39 miles and its width from north to south approximately 19 miles. The capital, Baria, was 68 miles by road from Saigon. The Task Force base at Nui Dat was some 12 miles north of Baria.

Phuoc Tuy was important to the government of Vietnam because National Route 15 provided the only land access from Saigon to the alternate port and resort centre of Vung Tau. Route 15 is the main highway linking Saigon, Baria and Vung Tau. Owing to its strategic significance it had already been the scene of considerable military activity during the First Indo-China War (1946–54). Then the beach resort had been a popular rest area for the French Army, and, it was claimed, for the Viet Minh. This situation repeated itself during the war against the Viet Cong, although now the inhabitants of the rest centres were American, Australian, New Zealand, South Korean, Thai and, most likely, some Viet Cong.

The terrain in Phuoc Tuy was typically flat, although there were three significant mountainous areas that dominated the countryside. These mountains were the Nui Thi Vai, Nui Din and Nui Toc Tien in the south-west, the Long Hai in the south and the Nui Mao Tai in the north-east. Besides these mountains there were a number of low extinct volcanic cones dotted throughout the province.

The low-lying south-western shoreline, bordering the South China Sea and the Saigon River estuary, was swampy and interlaced with waterways navigable by small watercraft. This region was known as the Rung Sat. The jungle tracks in the west, north and east of the province had many thickly vegetated gullies and ravines. Dense natural or cultivated vegetation covered most of the province except for small areas along the coastal belt where there was little or no vegetation at all. Mangrove covered the lower swampy areas of the Rung Sat. Heavy growth of trees, bamboo, shrubs, ferns and grasses covered the other areas.

Rubber plantations were scattered throughout the central and northern areas and covered some 30 square miles. The two largest plantations were the Courtenay rubber and the Binh Ba rubber. Most of the agricultural area was open to civilian access between the hours of 6am and 7pm each day. Generally, the civil access area lay astride the national and provincial highways from Phu My in the west to Xuyen Moc in the east and from Baria to the Courtenay rubber plantation in the north. The remainder of the terrain in the province was closed to civilian access and was treated by the Allies as a free fire zone. That is, fire could be opened against any person entering this area. Due care had to be taken along the boundaries of the zone because of the danger to civilians who might have strayed.

The rules of engagement here and within the civilian access area at night were designed to provide protection to the innocent.

The enemy main force unit in the province was the headquarters and one company of D65 North Vietnamese Army Engineer Battalion consisting of approximately 50 members. This unit normally operated in the Nui Thi Vai hills and in the north-western section of the province. Its main area of interest was along Route 15. Its principal method of operation was to wage mine warfare against the lines of communication. Also operating in the province was the D440 Local Force battalion consisting of a headquarters and two companies, a total of around 100 members. D440 had a hard core of North Vietnamese soldiers supplemented by some Viet Cong.

On 26 May 1970 the ANZAC Battalion moved out into the jungle: Operation *Capricorn*. Unknown to us at the time, this would be our only battalion-wide operation of the tour. This operation was a settling-in exercise to familiarise the more recent additions to the battalion, including my own company, with reconnaissance and ambush techniques in theatre. Another key aim of the operation was to re-establish the Australian presence to the west of Route 2. This area had been the responsibility of two US infantry battalions since January. On Operation *Capricorn* all five rifle companies were deployed together in one general area with a single task to find and destroy the enemy within that area of operations. This area was between the Nui Thi Vai and Nui Toc Tien mountains, in the hills and on the flat ground between the two features. This area extended from Route 15 to the Hat Dich area in the north. Battalion headquarters would control and direct the operation from Firebase Nola which would be established in the initial stage of the operation. The position chosen for the firebase had to be within 105mm howitzer range of companies operating between Route 15 and the northern boundary of the area of operations. The gun position ideally needed to be on open ground. This would also make it unnecessary to clear trees to fire the guns. The ideal location was identified as an area of raised ground between the Suoi Chau Pha and the Suoi Giao Keo river complexes.

Both the D440 Viet Cong Local Force Battalion and D65 North Vietnamese Army Engineer Battalion were known to be operating in the area. But there had been no contact with either for some months prior to the start of the operation.

On the morning of 26 May 1970 we were the first company to fly in and secure the area designated for Firebase Nola. Prior to our arrival the area was prepared by ground-attack aircraft dropping bombs, then artillery preparation from 105mm howitzers, then helicopter gunships, and finally we flew in on troop 'slicks'. But nobody had warned us that, as a matter of course, the door gunners would open fire as we descended into the landing zone. As the door gunners opened up we all got a hell of a fright and assumed that we were going into a hostile reception. However, the DZ was clear and we soon secured it and set off on our patrol tasks while the rest of the battalion flew in. With the firebase secure our goal was now to look after the northern slopes of Nui Thi Vai and Nui Toc Tien and the re-entrant between them.

After this startling introduction to our first combat helicopter insertion my platoon deployed from the LZ to cover our section of the company perimeter pushing some 20 yards into the jungle. Once the company was complete on the ground, which took about 30 minutes, each platoon deployed to its designated area of operations, leaving company HQ and a protection element in the vicinity of the LZ. 3 Platoon deployed north-west towards the slopes of the southern 'Wolvertons'. The other platoons of the company deployed north and north-east of the insertion LZ. The jungle we were now operating in was primary with low undergrowth and we moved slowly and carefully. For the next days we continued patrolling our area coming across old tracks and several disused bunker systems containing T-shaped bunkers with small perimeter trench systems. There was no recent sign of the enemy. The atmosphere within the platoon was tense and expectant as everyone moved silently through the low scrub. There was also an element of excitement – we were finally on a combat patrol in a VC area. We had rations and water for a week or so and so our packs, with rations, ammunition, grenades and claymores weighed 60–70 pounds, more for the two radio operators, three M79 grenadiers (who also carried an SLR), and three section machine gunners. In the field we wore floppy jungle hats and green denims or 'JGs' as we called them. We only wore our helmets and body armour as additional protection in static fire support bases. Our progress, deliberately, was slow and methodical and we covered about a 'click' (a kilometre) per hour with resting and listening breaks each hour or so. If the jungle became thicker the lead scouts would use garden secateurs to silently clear their routes. We did not use machetes or 'golloks' as we called them, as they were too noisy. Also, two members of each section carried small bush saws. Each night we established a defensive triangular position with platoon HQ in the centre. We would dig shell scrapes, which are shallow shelters in the ground for one man to lie in protected, about 18 inches deep, and lay out claymores in front of each section. At each apex of the platoon triangle the machine gunners would prepare their arcs of fire. Thirty minutes before and after dawn and dusk we had 'stand to' with each pair of men alert in their own shell scrape. This was a time of particular alertness and signalled the change from day routine to night routine and vice versa. Eating and night administration was completed before evening 'stand-to' and eating and day preparation was completed after the morning 'stand-to'. The various daily situation reports (SITREP) required by company HQ would be quietly transmitted just before the evening 'stand-to'.

On 29 May the battalion faced the menace of Viet Cong mines for the first time. Two separate mine incidents caused casualties in both Whisky Company and Charlie Company. In the Whisky Company incident tripwires detonated two grenades suspended in the tree, killing one soldier and wounding another. In Charlie Company the command detonation of an enemy claymore mine killed two soldiers and injured three others.

Generally, when contacted the enemy moved rapidly away and re-established themselves in a new area. During the first two weeks of our operations there were ten contacts with the enemy and the companies and battalion headquarters learned a great deal. The presence and locations of D65 were confirmed and evidence of its intention to operate against the government pacification programme and disrupt the civilian and military lines of communication along Route 15 was obtained from captured documents. While D440 remained elusive we soon found evidence of Chau Duc Local Force headquarters, which had a long history of operations in the province and was well known to 2 RAR veterans of their first tour in Vietnam (1967–68).

In early June 1970 elections were to be held throughout South Vietnam and the danger that orderly voting would be disrupted by Viet Cong military activities or terrorism brought a change in the concept of the Task Force operations. This was reflected in the new operation, *Chung Chung*, meaning 'Togetherness', which gave the battalion new tasks of preventing the enemy gaining access to the principal villages along Route 15. Rifle companies moved to areas astride and adjacent to Route 15. Battalion headquarters moved to a newly established Firebase Tess beside Route 15 and on the edge of the mangrove swamps of the Rung Sat. At the end of June most of the battalion returned to Nui Dat for two weeks of retraining and consolidation of lessons learned: lessons such as the effective use of artillery fire support and helicopter gunships; mine detection revision; medical evacuation procedures; major trauma and gunshot wound first aid; working with armoured vehicles; and for officers and SNCOs' revision on the use of the battalion report aide-memoire.

———

By mid-July when the unit was again ready to redeploy, the wet season had arrived in full and Firebase Tess had all but disappeared under the mud. With the clear identification of the area east of Phu My and Route 15 as an enemy base, resupply area and courier route the Task Force commander decided to conduct engineer land-clearing operations.

A detachment from 17 Construction Squadron, Royal Australian Engineers trained in the operation of heavy plant machinery would carry out the clearing. Four giant Rome ploughs would push over the vegetation and collect it into long windrows which could then be burned off in the next dry season when the wood had dried out. A troop of tanks and a section of APCs with this group would provide close protection for the land clearing team (LCT) and a rifle company would patrol the area around the worksite and also establish defensive positions at night.

The land-clearing operation was a tremendous task that would take several months to complete. The aim of the operation was to clear a large tract of land 12 square miles to the east of Phu My. The key purpose of clearing this forest was to deprive D65, North Vietnamese Engineer Battalion, of the use of an area in which it had operated in the past and in which it was beginning to show some interest again. The enemy, no longer protected and camouflaged by the thick jungle, would become vulnerable to observation when moving between his bases and his sources of supply. Also, once the conflict was over the local people could open up the area for farming and it would become beneficial to the economy of the province.

Our company was deployed east of Phu My off Route 15 in the low scrub and jungle around the foothills of the Wolverton Mountains. Highway 15 went from Saigon in the north-west to Vung Tau in the south about 60 miles away. We had been operating in the area for approximately ten days and our task was to intercept Viet Cong moving from the mountains into the villages along the highway. We had been in-country only about four weeks and this was our first time in this particular area. We were operating in platoon-sized patrols of about 30 men, which would then operate in ten-man squads. We had not had any contacts so far, so we were anxious to be blooded ourselves having been fed a diet of war stories ever since we stepped off our C-130 Hercules at Vung Tau.

We patrolled slowly with our trained lead scouts well forward. We had all been together for nearly a year and so our drills were well honed. We operated differently to the American, South

Vietnamese, Thai and Korean forces, who would go and find the Viet Cong and once they found them would 'pile on'. Due to our reduced numbers, our techniques, like the Australians', were more subtle.

We knew that with our superior firepower, as at least three of my guys carried the M79 grenade launcher, or 'duck gun', we could easily take on the Viet Cong if contact was made. What really worried us was the threat of mines that we knew were scattered liberally throughout this particular area.

We had been issued with maps of the area, and each mine incident was well marked. In some areas on the map you simply couldn't see the ground features for the number of spots denoting a mine incident. We knew the D65 North Vietnamese sappers were experts at laying mines and booby-traps. Whenever possible we never moved on tracks, which were the obvious place to put mines, but sometimes this was unavoidable due to the terrain or the noise that we made beating through the jungle. If we had to move on or near a track, then we would keenly search for the mine signs that the Viet Cong left for their own men.

There was a real art to carrying your equipment, ammunition, rations, bedding and water as well as always ensuring that your personal weapon was ready to fire. As a platoon commander I also carried a strobe light for night identification for aircraft, and the navigation equipment such as maps and a compass and pace-counter, as well as a small plastic-covered aide-memoire notebook containing the various radio formats for reporting a contact, mines, enemy sighting, bunkers or anything else of significance. We also each carried a shell dressing, a big bandage in a water-proof wrapper, taped on the butt of our weapons or on the bipod leg of the section machine guns. From experience we had learned that this was the best place to have the dressing, not in a pouch or a pocket, because if a man was shot or blown up it was easier to quickly locate the dressing as the weapon was normally lying near to the casualty. As well as the eight magazines in my ammunition pouches I carried two 20-round magazines on my M16 taped side-by-side. We did not have any 30-round magazines and anyway, the smaller magazines allowed me to get closer to the ground when returning fire in a contact. The second round in each magazine was a tracer round for target indication and the last two or three rounds were also tracer to remind you it was getting time to reload!

I personally carried an A-frame bergen rucksack with a large piece of brown foam rubber, liberated from a camp mattress, cushioning the pack on my back. Unfortunately, towards the end of my tour this pack finally rotted and fell apart. After that I had to try to fit everything into a much smaller issue pack.

We mainly carried New Zealand or Australian ration packs and these had a number of tins. Prior to each operation or after a resupply in the field we would go through all the ration packs we were issued and only keep the essential items. We carried out our rubbish whenever we could so that the enemy was not able to use any of it, such as empty tins, to make into booby-traps. The VC frequently used red Japanese mackerel tins filled with explosive as anti-personnel mines activated by bicycle batteries! Occasionally, we were issued with American rations which were very generous but far too big and we could only use a small amount of the contents. However, the US long range patrol (LRRP) rations were very light as they were dehydrated but we could only use them in the wet season when it rained heavily each day because they required lots of water to reconstitute the meals. Most of my soldiers would purchase instant noodles to take on patrol as these were light, tasty and filling and seasoned by small bottles of chilli sauce.

We cooked on small solid-fuel cookers, using hexamine blocks. Unfortunately, these gave off a slight odour and so we could only use them in certain tactical situations. If we could not use them, then we would eat our rations cold. We also learned the trick of quickly making a brew of tea or heating up a tin of food by using some of the US C4 plastic explosive we all carried. A small pellet of this malleable white explosive, like plasticine, would burn fiercely with little smell. I would place a small amount inside the 'V' of my detachable M16 bipod which was an ideal stove.

We generally all carried a pound of C4 in order to blow any unexploded shells or bombs we came across so that the Viet Cong could not extract the explosives from them to make into mines and booby-traps. We obviously only disposed of this ordnance if the situation permitted it – otherwise I would send a 'Mine Rep' (mine report) or 'Bomb Rep' (bomb report) to the company headquarters and at some time in the future the engineers could destroy it.

On 18 June the company had its first major action – a bloody introduction to the Vietnam War. 2 Platoon under my friend Ian Glendenning came across an enemy bunker system. While they were investigating the outskirts of the complex they were engaged by small arms fire and then a booby-trapped 155mm shell was detonated which killed two New Zealanders and wounded five others. Ian withdrew and called in fire support from armed helicopters. The Viet Cong group, which was about platoon strength, also withdrew. From this action, two soldiers in Ian's platoon were awarded Military Medals.

My platoon was nearby and later that day we proceeded to clear the enemy camp. We moved extremely cautiously into the camp area with two sections 'up' and one in reserve and I was behind the lead sections. We passed the bloodstained and disturbed ground from the initial contact and the area still smelt of cordite and explosives. The mini-gun fire from the helicopter gunships had stripped all the leaves from the trees and they lay on the ground like a carpet. There was a well in the centre of the camp complex into which I had the satisfaction of dropping a grenade in case there were any VC hiding there.

At one stage my signaller, Mike Anderson, and I realised that we were alone in the middle of the enemy camp – the two lead sections were sweeping forward and the reserve section was clearing the rear of the camp. The bush in the camp had silently absorbed some 30 Kiwi soldiers.

There were in fact two camps. One was 150 metres by 150 metres with five grass huts as well as over seven 2-metre by 2-metre bunkers, each with 1 metre of overhead protection. Nearby was another camp 100 metres by 100 metres with a 2-foot deep crawl trench around the perimeter. Both camps were protected by 105mm shells which could be command detonated. Each bunker had its own cooking area and bamboo dining table plus a tin containing chopsticks, toothbrushes and spoons. The bunkers also contained hammocks. In the centre of the camp on one of the bamboo tables were pots of cooked bamboo shoots – a smell which I have never forgotten – and on another table were seven M79 grenade rounds in the process of being made into booby-traps. We also found four 5-pound blocks of Chicom (Chinese communist) explosives.

1 Platoon under Roger M also had a contact shortly after this incident, on the evening of 28 June. However, to the amusement of the rest of the battalion the 'enemy' turned out to be two cows. Incidents like this at least kept our spirits up especially after we had suffered our first casualties.

The next operation we participated in was Operation *Nathan* from 13 July to 2 August. This new operation was a fourfold mission and saw the battalion becoming responsible for the security of the entire province to the west of and including Route 15; interdiction of enemy routes to the villages near Route 2; protection of engineer road reconstruction parties; protection of the LCT east of Route 15; and destruction of D65 Engineer Battalion. The Victor Company task was to take responsibility for base defence until July 17 and then begin reconnaissance and ambush operations in the surrounding area.

On 21 July I had my own very real, very personal introduction to the reality of war in Vietnam. We had been patrolling the jungle for about two days, slowly moving through the wet clawing bush paralleling a large sandy track that we knew was being used for infiltration by the enemy. The lead scouts indicated by hand sign that we had reached a large track junction. As it was getting late in the day I decided that this would be a suitable position to lay a night ambush. Every night on patrol we would set up a triangle harbour or defensive position. Each man except the gunners and radio operators would carry a claymore directional anti-personnel mine. We would position these mines to fire along any tracks we found.

The mines were placed to fire down the tracks so that maximum use was made of their 700 ball bearings. The platoon took up positions of all-round defence and one of the lead scouts and I went to check any likely approach routes from the mountains. We had only gone about 150 yards when the silence was torn by the distinctive sound of an M60 machine gun firing a long burst closely followed by the thudding of an SLR. There was an extremely brief return of fire from an AK-47 and then silence.

My immediate thought was that I had missed out on the platoon's first firefight so the scout and I sprinted back to the position, warning the sentry in a loud whisper that we were on our way back in. The body of one very dead Viet Cong lay in the bushes beside the track. There was also an AK-47 and an SKS rifle on the ground. My troop sergeant had organised a sweep of the area to ensure we had not missed anybody and I sent a contact report to the company commander back at headquarters in FSB Tess with the details of the contact. The clearing patrol came back and told me about two heavy blood trails they had found leading off towards the dark shape of the mountains. I quickly sent an artillery fire mission to our artillery support base, which was near the main highway. It was getting too dark for a follow-up so I ordered in some 105mm shells in the direction of the enemy's likely withdrawal route. A few minutes later the shells came whistling over our heads to land with a frightening crump in the jungle about 500 yards away. We all cringed, automatically glad that we were not on the receiving end of the tearing, ripping shrapnel from the artillery rounds.

We searched the body and removed items of intelligence value. He had been carrying a crude little medal presumably for bravery. He had also been carrying a small plastic pouch of cooked rice and bamboo shoots, in addition to extra magazines for his weapon in canvas chest webbing and a small medical kit containing ampoules of vitamin B. There was no sign of their normal sleeping gear of hammocks and plastic ponchos so we knew their base could not be more than 6–9 miles away.

It was too late to bury the corpse so we dug shell scrapes and established our night routine. This involved sentries at each of the machine gun positions which changed over every two hours. It was one of the scariest nights I have ever spent. We had the three sentry locations, one on each corner of our triangle position. One of these was only about 10 feet from the dead body. There was a slight moon, just enough to cause shadows on the white sandy track in front. We did sentry duty in staggered pairs and when I was silently woken I took my place in the shell scrape beside the machine gun and the claymore firing devices known as 'clackers'. I could not keep my eyes from straying back to the stiffening figure. But as I looked the body seemed to move and I could feel the hair on the back of my neck rising. I nudged my companion and pointed slowly. I need not have bothered. His eyes were riveted on the body too. We both knew he was dead, really dead, but still, the body was definitely moving. I slid one of the fragmentation grenades into my hand and prepared to pull the pin. We would not fire the M60 just yet as we needed to conceal its location for as long as possible. But what were we firing at – a moving corpse? Then out from underneath the body, moving slowly and awkwardly, came a huge iguana lizard. This one had obviously been doing some exploring. My hand, which had been gripping the gunner's arm in a vice-like grip to tell him when to fire, relaxed. We exchanged sheepish grins, and without a word passing between us we both knew that this was to be our little secret. Nobody would believe just how frightened we had been, and we weren't about to tell them.

At first light, a Sioux helicopter flew above our position to lower down a Polaroid camera to photograph the body and to take back the equipment and documents to the intelligence section at Nui Dat. We took the required 'mugshot' as quickly as possible, dismissed the chopper, buried the late Viet Cong and set off along the valley towards the centre of the Wolvertons. This was where the blood trails and drag marks had led.

If anything, movement was even more cautious than before the contact. We were following wounded men and every hollow in the ground, thick bush or rock was a potential ambush site. The tracks were leading us further and further into those forbidding mountains. My map, which showed locations of previous mine incidents, was covered in red dots along the area we were travelling. Suddenly, the lead scout froze and pointed to the left of the track. In the branch of a small tree about 6 inches above the ground was a small piece of torn yellow cloth, invisible to the eye of the untrained. It was a mine sign! Passing right beside the cloth the trails of slowly drying blood carried on up the steepening slope towards large, dark grey boulders crouching in the thickening jungle.

'Mines,' the urgent whisper came down the column. 'Sign on the left!' Walking as if on eggshells, eyes scanning every inch of the ground the platoon moved painfully slowly forward. The lead scouts had the doubly difficult task of following the blood trails and also looking for likely enemy positions. We were slowly being drawn into the heart of the dark forbidding Wolverton Mountains.

We came to where there was a larger blood trail and we saw that the wounded or one of the wounded had given themselves an injection of vitamin B. We pushed on for several days. The terrain was now much narrower by this point and the blood trail was following a stony dry stream bed that weaved in between the rocks and the trees. We were moving in single file, but with two men on each side to cover our flanks. I had moved an M60 machine gun behind the scouts so that they would have immediate rapid-fire support if we were attacked. At intervals we would silently adopt a defensive position and while half of the group watched the perimeter the other half opened cans of C rations and packets of military biscuits. There was no question of heating the food on our little hexamine stoves or even boiling water for a 'brew'. This was 'Indian country' and even the faint odour of the burning dry fuel blocks ran the risk of giving away our present location. After each break I gave the signal and we would quietly slip our packs on our shoulders and move off following the trail of blood as it went up the hill. The threat of mines on the riverbed was slim because of the difficulty of concealment, but tripwires were a source of concern. The lead scout held a small stick between the fingers of his left hand at knee height. If the twig hit a tripwire it was not large enough to break the wire and detonate a booby-trap but it would alert the scout to the danger. Progress was incredibly slow, but we knew the skilful reputation of our sapper enemy.

The burst of fire on the trail above caught us by surprise and every man flung himself to the ground throwing off his main pack. The shooting was an M16, ours, and was followed by the distinctive cracking explosions of an M79 grenade. The lead scout of the point section, Bill T, was in action! The thumping of the cover scout's SLR added to the din echoing around the rocks and trees. The words 'Contact front – two enemy!' were passed down the column. A third weapon fired and the characteristic rattle of an AK-47 sent bullets cracking through the trees above our heads. The warning that the enemy was throwing grenades was made unnecessary by the explosions around us. The Viet Cong were on a small plateau in the rocks above us and we could hear their urgent chatter.

The platoon had automatically moved into fire positions covering front and to the flanks. I clearly remember noticing, as we were sorting out our fire positions, that a number of my soldiers were smoking. Smoking in the jungle was always strictly controlled because the smell could alert any nearby enemy. I was annoyed by it then, immediately, I knew the ridiculousness of my thoughts: the enemy knew where we were – they were shooting at us!

The lead section was exchanging fire with the hidden enemy who had us at a territorial disadvantage. As I crawled forward, to find out the situation, the lead scout, Bill T, who was attached to my platoon from the NZSAS troop in Nui Dat, crawled back to brief me. 'This is the camp, boss, and there are two sentries. I think I hit one. There is a massive boulder behind them, and I saw more movement there.'

At this moment there was a lull in the battle and I became very aware that all my soldiers near me were looking directly at me. I was the leader – this was what it was all about – all the months I had spent being taught and practising being an officer now had to be put into action.

I briefed the artillery officer, located at the company headquarters, on my radio and requested an immediate fire mission and gunship support. I knew we were right on the edge of the enemy camp and would have to bring the artillery shells in 'danger close'. If we moved back down the hill the Viet Cong would escape to the north. 'Shot over!' came the gunner's response. The shells were on their way from the 105mm howitzers located in the FSB beside Highway 15 to the east of our location.

Then our world exploded! We were thrown into the air by the explosions. Shrapnel, stones, debris flew everywhere. It was the loudest noise I had ever heard. A salvo of three shells had smashed into the rocks just in front of us. 'Check firing! Check firing!' I screamed into the radio. I knew another salvo was about to arrive and we would not survive that. I explained the situation to the gunner officer, and he said that the howitzers were at the maximum angle due to the steepness of the valley we were in and could not be adjusted further.

The cavalry was coming – the gunships I had requested were on their way and they would sort out these 'Charlies'. 'Hello India Four-Three, this is Albatross Zero One. I have rockets and mini-guns where you want them?' Let me tell you there is nothing quite as reassuring as the sound of gunships rolling in and 'brassing up' the jungle. The three gunships, a heavy fire team, took it in turns to fly towards the mountains, just below the mist, firing everything they had before pulling up with inches to spare. Bits of rocket crashed through the canopy above our heads and red-hot cartridge cases rained down among us. For 20 minutes these flying dragons spewed flame and destruction into the rocks above us. The canopy was stripped bare and the pungent stink of cordite was everywhere. Then the choppers wheeled away. While the gunships were strafing the area ahead of us, I was kneeling beside a large rock, controlling proceedings, and the rifle sections waited in all-round defence. The rest of my platoon HQ was in cover behind other boulders. Almost in slow motion I watched a grenade thrown by the VC above me sail over the rock and land with a plop on the ground about 10 feet away from me. I stared at it horrified and then forced myself as deep into the ground as possible. Nothing happened! I studied the grenade and saw it was a US M67 'egg-shaped' fragmentation grenade and it was tightly wrapped in black tape – which is why it did not explode. I mentally thanked the US GI who had lost that grenade for covering it with black tape – as was their habit.

The artillery shells had landed very near to us and, as well as enemy grenade fragments several of my soldiers had received minor shrapnel wounds and damaged eardrums from the artillery blasts. The enemy was silent and we could no longer detect any movement so I arranged for the medical evacuation 'dust-off' helicopters to come and winch these men, including Bill T, out of the jungle.

Once the choppers departed there was an eerie silence. Cautiously, I moved towards the lead section. Each man tucked into a rocky crevice. A quick word to the commander and they adjusted positions to cover the reserve section moving through them as we moved into the camp area amongst small caves. We came across a scene of desolation – there was nothing left standing. All the undergrowth had been stripped away by rockets and mini-gun fire, some of it only 20 feet in front of our positions. Leaves covered the ground and a thick brown carpet of branches and wood splinters lay everywhere. In the centre was a clump of grey boulders chipped and splintered. We continued upwards, and in the middle of a small clearing saw what had once been a kitchen area. Pots and pans and bamboo lay scattered on the ground. A steel container of rice had been hit by a cannon shell and was lying leaking on its side. The rice was still warm. At that stage during this contact we had been supported by 105mm howitzers from Phu My and US 8-inch guns from Nui Dat; and, to my surprise a Centurion tank moving along the Firestone Trail on the flat land below us contacted me and assisted by firing shells into the hillside above us. I never found out where that tank came from or where it was going to!

We had not found any enemy casualties in the camp and so we hoped to continue to follow their trail. But it suddenly became clear that this would not be an option. The camp itself was mined! We were literally standing in the middle of a minefield. The impersonal booby-trap or mine that killed or horribly mutilated victims was something we all feared. A firefight was different – you took your chances and so did the enemy – but mines … In the words of Field Marshal Sir William Slim: 'Everything that is shot or thrown at you, or dropped on you in war is most unpleasant, but of all the horrible devices the most terrifying … is the landmine.'

Only a unit with the expertise of these North Vietnamese sappers would consider mining the interior of their own camp. The first mine that exploded seriously injured three men. The mine had been located where I had been standing just minutes before. To this day I do not know how I did not tread on it! But before I could do anything a second mine exploded. This second mine seriously damaged the lower legs of one soldier and injured several others. The third explosion was shielded by rocks and thankfully only stunned people. To make matters worse, the wounds caused were made even more horrific because the mines, in individual mackerel tins, had been surrounded by glass bottles. Glass is difficult to identify on X-rays, making the surgeon's job even more challenging. But first I had to get my injured men out of the minefield and onto the surgeon's operating table.

Being inside a minefield is a nightmare experience and your instinct is to just freeze – every footstep you take may be your last before you die in a violent explosion. But when you have your dazed and bloodied soldiers around you badly needing life-saving first aid you have to override your fear. I spoke firmly to those near me and ordered them to stand on rocks, not on the naked earth. Hopping from rock to rock I quickly went to one of the badly injured, Ruka H, lying motionless on the rocky ground, moaning quietly. His legs were badly mutilated and he was losing a lot of blood through his wounds. I made a tourniquet out of my sweat rag, tied it around his thigh and tightened it using a small wooden branch to twist the rag. I can still clearly remember the squishing sound the damaged flesh made as I tightened the tourniquet. Sergeant Beattie was attending to one of the other serious casualties. I had already requested another 'dust-off' helicopter and it was soon hovering above us.

Those not involved in the casualty evacuation moved cautiously into fire positions to ensure that the North Vietnamese could not fire at the vulnerable 'dust-off' helicopter. There was no suitable landing zone so the helicopter had to hover some distance away from the cliff face we were now on. A Stokes litter was lowered and we gently placed one casualty in it. This litter is like a stretcher and the casualty is laid inside it and strapped in, after which the winch cable is connected to the top end of the stretcher. I assisted the litter as it was winched from the big rock on which some of us were positioned but eventually I had to let go and the casualty swung out over the treacherous drop below us before being safely hauled on board. We did the same for the next casualty but when I released him I had to watch horrified as he swung straight into the trunk of a tree opposite us. He was vertical in his stretcher and I could see his face clearly as he hit the tree – his expression never changed but his bloodied foot turned almost completely around. He swung away from the tree and was quickly winched into the helicopter, as were the other casualties, and they were flown straight to the main evacuation hospital at Vung Tau. The remainder of us, only two thirds of the original platoon, now moved slowly, very slowly back down the mountain and established a night harbour in a rocky stream bed, just over a mile away from the contact area. We carried the equipment of the medevaced wounded with us so the enemy could not retrieve it. Our casualties survived and some returned to the platoon but Ruka H had both legs amputated and 'Doc' Takuta had one leg removed. Very soon, once they were stabilised, they were evacuated back to their families in New Zealand.

Those of us who remained carried on with our tour but now with even greater purpose. Over the next few weeks we moved back to the same cave system near the camp we had attacked but this time approached from the high ground above. A heavy bombing raid was delivered onto the area of the caves before we entered it and we lay huddled amongst the massive rocks on the top of the mountain as the jets screamed on their bombing runs just above our heads. The earth shuddered as the bombs exploded and we were hammered by the over-pressure of the blasts.

When the jets had left, the air stank of explosives. The rocks in the area of the caves were smashed and battered. As we moved closer we came across the pathetic sight of a large monkey, undamaged but quite dead, hanging above us by one arm from one of the few remaining trees. We checked the area as best we could and then withdrew. The enemy had long gone.

In the subsequent weeks I was patrolling with my platoon to the west of Route 2. I was covering the southern part of our platoon patrol area and Sergeant Beattie had moved to the northern area. On 28 September he had a very successful ambush which accounted for five enemy dead and one wounded. His half-platoon patrol identified some fresh tracks, laid an ambush and engaged some ten enemy dressed in black clothing. The initial engagement counted for five dead and a clearing sweep located a wounded enemy. Gunships were called and engaged further enemy nearby but no further enemy casualties were located. I was extremely anxious to try to contact the VC fleeing from this ambush and moved north as quickly as possible to link up with the rest of my platoon. However, we did not have any contacts on the way. Undoubtedly, we were competitive amongst ourselves regarding the number of successful contacts. After all, this was what we were here to do. It is hard to describe the adrenalin rush of combat to the uninitiated.

Throughout 1–2 October we were cautiously following a very well defined enemy track through the jungle east towards Route 2. At approximately 10.30am on 2 October, we came across a large and recently occupied bunker complex. We had earlier come across felled trees with the stumps covered in mud to hide them from aerial observation. The trees were used for overhead protection of individual bunkers. There was also the smell of a latrine. This substantial defensive area could easily house at least 40 enemy combatants and it had clearly been in use in the past few days. Clearing that camp was probably one of the most unsettling periods of my entire tour in Vietnam. My skin prickled and I was expecting to be ambushed at any time.

We had thoroughly investigated the camp and continued in an eastwards direction towards Route 2 when we heard the sound of chopping. We crept forward and saw some locals, who were cutting fruit, talking to a group of men. We challenged them and suddenly saw that one had an M1 carbine which he pointed directly at us. We quickly spread out into line-abreast and put an immediate sweep line through the area. We knew we had wounded at least one by the clearly evident blood trail but they were all able to escape except the M1 carbine. As we were moving the sweep line I was beside the machine gunner, Harry E, and to his irritation I kept asking him to make sure that he had enough ammunition left. His M60 machine gun was called the 'Baron'. I was still very concerned that we would bump into the large group that I believed could still be in the area and we needed to have enough ammunition for a sustained battle. The enemy who escaped this initial contact ran straight past our last ambush position where my base was still located but, to my anger, my soldiers were not alert and did not open fire. Later, when we had re-formed back in the night ambush position, a woman came creeping down the track. The sentry on duty blew the claymore beside the track. Although totally stunned she was almost entirely uninjured thanks to her closeness to the claymore when it was fired. While we were giving her first aid we discovered a bag with a wig in it together with a substantial amount of money. She was evacuated with these items to Nui Dat by helicopter. Battalion intelligence later confirmed that she was a courier and that the others operating in the area were from the Chau Duc Viet Cong District headquarters.

The company moved back into the south-west area of the province and commenced patrolling. This was an area with which we were becoming familiar. On 31 October a half-platoon patrol from 1 Platoon, led by Lieutenant Roger M, was crossing the Suoi Cha Pha River. One of the patrol NCOs had an accidental discharge, killed one of their own and wounded two others. One was shot in the leg several times and one was shot in the jaw. These tragic events can and do happen in war, but Lieutenant M chose to conceal the events. When he returned to base some weeks later he wrote a false contact report complete with a map stating that they had been attacked, returned fire and followed a blood trail. His soldiers had to carry this secret with them for so many years at a huge mental cost to themselves. The family of the soldier who was killed never knew he had been accidentally killed by his own men until many years later. This was a tragic blue-on-blue incident.

———

The company was still operating in the enemy infiltration route area east of Phu My and on 4 November my platoon had another contact. We had established an ambush position beside a sandy track which looked as though it had been used fairly recently. The sentry position had to be close to the track because of the limited visibility in the thick bush beside the track. It also meant we had to be close to our claymores. At about midday the claymores exploded with a great roar as two Viet Cong had cautiously approached up the track. We quickly took up our stand-to positions. I crawled to the sentry team who were covered in dirt from the nearest claymore and somewhat deafened. The air reeked of burnt plastic — the distinctive smell when claymores are fired. The M60 let rip and I called up support from helicopter gunships. They soon arrived and opened fire up and down the track.

Afterwards we swept the area and located one dead Viet Cong and a blood trail from the other. We then spent a considerable amount of time looking for the wounded Viet Cong in the thick bush. We kept trying to get him to give up by shouting at him in Vietnamese to surrender – ‘*lai dai!*’ But no such luck. Eventually we were compelled to throw grenades into the area to force him out.

By this time it was dark and the battalion headquarters was demanding that we capture this enemy. An easy instruction to give when you are sitting on your fat arse in a deep dug-out. I requested artillery illumination, but this was denied, apparently because of the proximity to civilian habitation. Eventually a Pilatus Porter aircraft dropped flares to assist us, and two of my NCOs, Sandy Sandford and Johnnie Bluett, crept into the bush and located the Viet Cong who was lying on his hammock holding his AK-47. He was taken out by helicopter the next day with two or three M16 bullet wounds in his back from the original contact.

This was a hazardous task at night and I was unimpressed by the lack of artillery illumination support. I believed my soldiers had been placed at unnecessary risk.

A few days later we were in the same vicinity when we sited an ambush position beside one of these open areas with a track running through it. We saw movement down the track and waited expectantly. We soon realised that it was a 2 Platoon patrol moving very slowly down the track. I did not know why they were in our area. We let them come closer before we planned to make our presence known in case they suddenly opened fire. Their lead scout was directly in front of us when he must have seen a portion of one of the claymores covering the track – he froze and turned as white as a sheet. We quickly and quietly let him know we were there.

This incident emphasised how important accurate navigation was on any operation. Except in the open paddy fields or near the major roads, all navigation was conducted in thick jungle. It was almost impossible to locate any distinctive terrain features in the jungle. Map reading had to be excellent as we attempted to match up the contours with the surrounding geography. This was many years before the introduction of the GPS which makes navigation a breeze for today's soldiers. Combined with the map we used the robust and accurate military prismatic compass and the pace-counters taped onto our rifles. Most platoon commanders and platoon sergeants and many of the section commanders had pace-counters. Pace-counters were extremely useful for counting and recording distance walked by clicking the device on every second step – this was about one yard, depending upon the terrain. Accurate navigation undoubtedly helped keep my platoon and me alive.

The Australian battalion commanding officer, Lieutenant Colonel JC, always wore sunglasses and smoked big cigars. We all thought he had watched too many John Wayne films. On 9 November he was shot down while flying over the Rung Sat swamp area on the edge of our area of operations. He received a minor wound but guaranteed himself a Distinguished Service Order (DSO). Getting shot down but receiving only a minor injury (embarrassingly in his backside) must have been the answer to his prayers.

He and our OC, John Mc, did not seem to get on too well. I believe he felt John Mc was too laid back; he wrote in his book *Second to None*, 'I visited John Mc in his headquarters on the summit of Nui Toc Tien. I found him to be his usual laconic self ...'. Lieutenant Colonel JC made a point of visiting companies in the field on a regular basis using 'his' Sioux helicopter. I think he felt these visits were good for morale but we found them a pain in the arse. He would be more worried about whether troops had shaved than about the tactical situation. Moreover, his bloody helicopter made sure that our locations were obvious to any nearby Viet Cong. Whenever there was a contact and he was in the air he would appear above the area and make a total nuisance of himself!

He was highly critical of the use of artillery as cut-offs after a contact to engage likely enemy withdrawal routes and cause further casualties to them. He believed that this was a waste of resources. We soldiers on the ground disagreed but he criticised Victor 5 on more than one occasion for using artillery in this way after a contact. We firmly believed this was an effective method of engaging fleeing enemy soldiers. Also, in his book *Second to None*, he criticises me for bringing in artillery too close during my contact in the Nui Thi Vai Mountains – he was obviously unaware that the guns were on extreme elevation and that I had made a fully thought-out decision before requesting their fire support. I was the man on the ground!

There was even a lingering rumour that he was shot down by Kiwi troops who were exasperated by his constant meddling. It isn't true, of course, but we did share a few wry grins when it happened.

We were all allocated two periods of five-day leave during our 12-month tour. In December 1970 I was allocated a leave period and was due to join Cecilia in Singapore. I had come out of the field on a resupply chopper and I was in Nui Dat in our base area sitting in the officers' and senior NCOs' dining room on Christmas Day. I was to depart for my leave the following day. Suddenly, the silence of the evening was shattered by rifle fire coming from about 50 yards away from the building I was in. I quickly grabbed my rifle, turned off the light and crept towards the door. I thought that a Viet Cong sapper group had entered the camp. There was no more firing. Near our location inside the Nui Dat base was the sergeants' mess of the Royal Australian Army Service Corps (RAASC). The firing had come from this building. I went to assist and soon established that it had not been an enemy attack but that, after an all-day drinking session, an Australian private soldier, Ferriday, had taken his SLR, loaded a full magazine of live rounds and commenced to shoot, indiscriminately, into the RAASC sergeants' mess building. Two sergeants were killed, and one seriously wounded. The incident was especially tragic because those who were shot were due to return to Australia the following day after the completion of their 12-month service in Vietnam. Ferriday was later convicted on two counts of manslaughter and one of assault with a weapon and served eight years of a ten-year sentence. My Christmas leave had certainly started off in a dramatic fashion. Thankfully the rest of my leave was much calmer and quieter but it was over all too soon and Cecilia and I were faced with another difficult goodbye.

In February 1971 my company was located in the area around Firebase Garth in the north of the province and patrolling the area east of Route 2. This was not an area we were familiar with and it was very dense bush. Patrolling was exceptionally slow and cautious. We had to try to move as silently as possible through thick secondary jungle and large patches of bamboo. Bamboo is particularly noisy and physically difficult to get through and for this reason the Viet Cong often dug bunker systems around and in bamboo patches. Generally the company patrolled in platoon or half-platoon groups. Company HQ would move separately and was protected by a rotated half-platoon from one of the rifle platoons. If company HQ was static they would sometimes have a pair of 81mm mortars attached for fire support if we were out of the reach of artillery. I was part of the company headquarters protection during this operation with half of my platoon. I really resented being stuck with company headquarters and wanted to be out on the ground with my platoon. It was not a pleasant few weeks. The rest of my platoon under Sergeant Beattie had several contacts and that frustrated me even more. One such contact involved an RPG 2 round landing directly in front of one of the patrol machine gun positions. It blew the gun clean in half. The gunner himself was unwounded but more than a little startled! I was more than happy to get back out on the ground with my soldiers once my duties at company headquarters were complete.

When you are living in the jungle for long periods of time moving silently through the bush you are privileged to see a great deal of wildlife up close. There were the noisy hornbills who flew in the canopy above us but whose landing techniques were singularly unglamorous. They would literally crash into the foliage of trees, hang on tightly, and then sort out their feathers and get tidy again rather like embarrassed little old ladies who had taken a tumble. Mouse deer were my favourites. These were toy-sized deer stepping delicately through the bushes and, if you sat perfectly still, they would trot past within feet of you. The gibbon monkeys would 'whoop' as they moved through the trees swinging from branch to branch. They did cause us a few anxious moments. One night, at 'stand-to', we heard what sounded like an enemy 'sweep line' moving straight for our position and extending some distance on either side as it moved towards us. We awaited the onslaught, weapons with safety catches off, claymore safety bales lowered, grenades ready and getting as low as we could in our shell scrapes with just our noses poking out! The noise came closer and closer, but we couldn't see anything. Then suddenly the noise carried on over the top of us! It was a huge troop of monkeys moving determinedly through the treetops. We gave a collective silent sigh of relief and relaxed our tensed muscles.

The 'fuck you!' lizard was an interesting night companion. This lizard grew to about 3 feet long and at dusk would start its call which sounded just like someone saying, 'fuck you!' We grew used to this noise because it meant that there was no one around us.

If the lizards heard movement they went quiet. We were always aware of snakes, but they were usually desperately trying to get away from us.

At night, lying on the ground you would frequently hear termites digging and scratching beneath the piece of plastic you lay on. If you were unlucky and lay on a termite nest chunks of your plastic sheeting would be eaten by the morning. They also gave a very painful nip. Normally we would pour insect repellent or powder around the outside of the sleeping position to deter these vicious creepy crawlies. That piece of plastic was all we had for a peaceful night's sleep. We were issued with small blow-up mattresses, but these were too noisy to use out in the field and were only ever used inside large firebases. Some of the other platoon commanders permitted the use of hammocks but I wouldn't allow them in my platoon. In a contact, particularly at night, most soldiers fire high. If you are lying in a hammock and not on the ground, you are very vulnerable to incoming fire. Also, I found that night defensive positions tended to focus around suitable hammock trees and not on tactical security. I wanted to keep my soldiers alive and not shot, rather than comfortable at night.

We began to operate west of Firebase Garth, on the edge of the Courtenay rubber plantation, at the end of February. I liked this area. It was a popular infiltration route for the Viet Cong so contact with the enemy was always likely. On one day we were in a harbour position in some old rubber trees and secondary scrub. There was a single shot and then silence. We took cover and I tried to work out if we were in contact or not. There was no further shooting. I soon established that one of the two Australian engineers who were attached to my platoon had shot himself in the foot. I had to arrange for a dust-off helicopter to come and evacuate him.

While I was carrying out first aid on the soldier's gunshot wound he was in shock and kept mentioning his wife. I tried to reassure him that his wife would be contacted as soon as possible. This seemed to make him more and more agitated. It was only after he had been evacuated that I realised he had been asking me NOT to tell his wife!

On the night of 5 March, I established an ambush position with some of my platoon on the edge of the Viet Cuong rubber plantation, part of the huge Courtenay rubber plantation, with another ambush position from the platoon located some 2½ miles further to the east. Late in the evening we spotted movement coming from the west passing our position and continuing past some small derelict huts towards another village. Our position was too far away from the enemy route to be effective, so I instructed the patrol to disconnect their claymore firing devices and we moved out in light patrol order towards the enemy movement.

I had been carrying a US white phosphorous fragmentation grenade which I had managed to get my hands on. The rest of our grenades were basic fragmentation M26 grenades. When we were close to where we had seen movement, I whispered to the section commander to throw my grenade into the area where we thought the enemy was hiding to get them moving so we could see and shoot them. Corporal Johnnie Bluett was a big man and I knew he could hurl this particular grenade a long distance. At the same time one man in the patrol saw movement close to him and opened fire. The firing carried on punctuated by the impressive and lethal explosion of the white phosphorous grenade.

A light appeared in one of the huts nearby, so we engaged that with machine gun fire. We swept the area as best we could in the dark but did not find anything. A short time later we heard firing as my other ambush opened fire. We waited in the contact area and then made our way cautiously back to our original position. The next day a sweep revealed one dead Viet Cong together with his weapon and a small pack. The other ambush patrol had killed another Viet Cong.

Some years later at a company reunion, Jay Seymour, one of my soldiers from that ambush, confided in me that when he had seen the Viet Cong he had quickly advised his section commander. The section commander, Bluett, immediately told him, 'Don't tell the Boss – he will make us go after them!' He had to break the news that he had already told me and that, yes, we were going after them!

Patrolling did not always involve contact with the enemy and for some of our time in the jungle we did not come across any enemy or even any sign of the enemy. A lot of time was simply spent in ambushing any tracks or likely sign that we did find. It is difficult to ensure that there is no noise in an ambush that may go on for days. The soldiers would take paperback novels to read; Westerns, 'Yippees' as they were known, were very popular, but to cut down on weight each book would be torn into three or four sections. These bits would be randomly distributed amongst each section so that you could end up receiving any part of a book to read which was then swapped for another part.

I also permitted one or two small portable radios in each rifle section and on these we could listen to the US Armed Forces Radio (AFVN) using little earphones. The aim of these diversions was to keep the noise of whispering or any movement down to an absolute minimum.

On 10 March 1971, my good friend Lieutenant John Winton of 1 Platoon sadly died of injuries he received when a claymore detonated while he was sweeping a contact area. He had replaced Lieutenant M, who had been posted to the US base, Bearcat, north of Phuoc Tuy.

This was 1 Platoon's first successful enemy contact in ten months on operations. The sentry in the platoon ambush position had killed an approaching Viet Cong. John and two others had gone into the contact area to sweep for further enemy casualties. But the firing of the machine gun during the initial contact had set the dry grass ablaze. This in turn ignited the detonating cord which connected the claymore banks. A claymore detonated and John was caught in the blast. Another member of the patrol was also wounded. With the 'black humour' that soldiers in combat always have, 1 Platoon were called the 'Lovers' by the rest of the Company, not as a compliment about their more amorous activities in the flesh-pots of Vung Tau, but because they supposedly 'loved' the Viet Cong so much they did not want to kill them. Maybe 1 Platoon would have been more successful on operations if John Winton had not been killed – who knows!

After this latest operation we had our four-day rest-in-country at the Task Force leave centre in Vung Tau. I was sad about the death of John Winton, whose company I normally enjoyed when we were on leave in Vung Tau. I got 'wrecked' one night in the bars in Vung Tau town centre. This inevitably resulted in a confrontation with the obnoxious Australian military police (MP) at curfew time. I ended up being arrested, handcuffed and taken to the cells in Vung Tau base. I was gamely assisted by a number of my platoon who took exception to my arrest. At the resulting disciplinary hearing some weeks later in Nui Dat I had to defend my actions to the Task Force brigadier against the accusations of no fewer than nine MPs who had obviously made it their mission to get me into trouble. In Vietnam, most of the Australian MPs were policemen in normal life with no real understanding of the pressures of operational life in the field. The brigadier was very lenient when he realised the circumstances that had led to my behaviour.

I am not particularly proud of my actions that night and I suspect it cost me a Military Cross, but I still cannot stop a chuckle or two when I read the lengthy charge sheet against me. It includes me saying things to the MPs like: 'Fuck off you POGO bastards!' POGO is a highly derisory term given by a combat soldier to someone who does not go out on operations into the jungle, i e 'permitted on garrison only'.

The day of 20 March found us once again patrolling south-east of Firebase Garth in two separate patrol groups. I was in thick primary jungle and the other patrol was in part of the overgrown rubber plantation that was the huge Courtenay rubber complex. I received a radio call from the other patrol commander, a junior NCO, informing me that a body of Viet Cong was moving past his position. He thought there were at least 12. He finally opened fire on them but did not follow up. In the meantime, my patrol moved as quickly as possible towards the contact area, hoping to cut off this enemy group. We could not move through the bush very easily and so we did not see them at all. The other patrol received a minor casualty, most likely simply a ricochet from one of their own weapons. I was most unimpressed by the lack of aggression from this particular NCO.

On 22 April my platoon made its final kill when a Viet Cong trying to get past the platoon as we were moving at the rear of the company column was shot and killed by Mike 'Gwan Gwan' August, one of my scouts.

On 30 April the company returned to Nui Dat for the final time. We knew our return home was looming because we had been ordered to take our 'happy pills' for the previous two weeks. Malaria was endemic in Vietnam and we were required to take paludrine on a daily basis. As platoon commander it was my responsibility to ensure that we took our daily dose. I had to maintain a notebook on operations in which the names of all my soldiers were recorded and beside which I had to sign to say that each soldier had taken his paludrine. During our tour we were also given dapsone, a more powerful anti-malaria drug. The so-called 'happy pills' were designed to rid our bodies of the common types of malaria which had been suppressed by the regular paludrine pills. The 'happy pills' were chloroquine (a large pink pill) and primaquine (a small brown pill). They were called 'happy pills' because we were going home! This final cocktail of drugs really knocked us all about and, even though we were still on operations, some of my soldiers were not in a fit state for combat. One of the soldiers in my patrol, Bryce 'the man from Marble Mountain' Newlove, had carried an M72 portable rocket launcher on operation for many weeks. While we were waiting at the LZ for that final helicopter ride back into Nui Dat I told him to fire the launcher at a tree in the surrounding jungle. This he did with great pleasure. It was the final act of aggression by 3 Platoon, Victor 5 Company in Vietnam. I suppose I could always blame the 'happy pills' if reprimanded.

I had found operational soldiering exciting and challenging. Vietnam had provided me with the opportunity to command men under fire for the very first time and I had discovered that I was able to control my own fear when under fire. Jungle warfare without the sophistication of technology is one of the rawest operational environments in which to fight. As described by the legendary World War II Malaya jungle veteran Freddie Spencer Chapman DSO and Bar, the jungle is in essence neutral; it can be both your friend and your enemy, and acceptance of this is key to survival. In Vietnam all the officer and leadership training I had received up until this point had had to be put into play. During that first firefight in the Nui Thi Vai Mountains I had felt the stares of my men on me. The jungle presents a multitude of places to hide, but there was nowhere to hide from the gaze of the men I commanded – even if I had wanted to! In my platoon we suffered wounds and injuries but we all made it home alive – a fact that I am incredibly proud of.

I respected our enemy there in Vietnam, as I have generally always respected my enemy. (This was not the case when I served in Northern Ireland – I loathed and despised the IRA and their ilk and I still do.) However, I have noticed that there is a move afoot to get together with former enemy soldiers from our combat days in Vietnam. This initiative seems to have originated amongst Australian Vietnam veterans. I have no interest whatsoever in making friends with former NVA and Viet Cong against whom I was fighting. I am just rather disappointed that my platoon and I were not able to kill more than we did. They were trying to maim or kill us and we were trying to do the same to them. In our particular case – we just did it better!

Such is war. I make no apologies for being an aggressive soldier. For me there is no point being a combat soldier without some level of aggression. I was given the epithet 'Warry Mac' by my soldiers in Vietnam and it is a nickname that I carry with great pride – and a certain amount of embarrassment.

The New Zealand infantry is extremely proud of the part it played in South Vietnam and even though the New Zealand contribution was small in terms of manpower, it was big in terms of operational efficiency.

RETURN TO SINGAPORE

I returned with the company to Singapore in May 1971 and was then posted to the Support Company as the battalion signals officer. I had completed a basic officers' signals course in NZ, though I was never much of a signaller and persevered mainly by bluffing my way. My biggest problem was operating the huge combination lock on the bloody great safe in battalion headquarters where the communication codes were secured.

Before we left Vietnam our Victor 5 Company second-in-command, Captain Alvin Clement, had discreetly told me I had been recommended for a Military Cross (MC). Several months after I had returned to Singapore I was called in to see the commanding officer, Lieutenant Colonel Rob W (later to become Chief of the New Zealand General Staff, 1981–84). He congratulated me and told me I had been awarded a Mention in Dispatches (MiD) for gallantry during my tour in South Vietnam. This was a great honour and I was very proud, but I have to admit some disappointment that my award was not an MC. Many years later I wrote to our company commander from our Vietnam days, John Mc, and asked him if he had indeed recommended me for an MC. He wrote back and confirmed that he had but that it had been downgraded by the Australians because there were limitations on how many could be issued – two Australian officers from our ANZAC Battalion were awarded MCs.

Naturally my father found the situation ironic considering he had been in a very similar position during World War II. He was also recommended for an MC and despite receiving three MiDs his commanding officer told him that 'his' MC was to be given to a regular officer not a battlefield commission like my father – but he was sure my father would understand!

I was more disturbed by my active service in Vietnam than I realised, and I became very distant from Cecilia who had been waiting so long for me to safely return from Vietnam. She could not understand why I was so different and she was very hurt. Quite simply I just wanted to be with the men I served with. I gather my state of mind was a common syndrome. I had been working closely with my men through thick and thin for some 12 months. I found settling back into domestic life as well as routine barrack life very difficult.

We did not receive any counselling when we returned from Vietnam, or the offer of any, but I suspect I would not have been willing to accept any support even if it had been available.

LEAVING THE NEW ZEALAND ARMY 1973

We returned to New Zealand in December 1971 and I was promoted to captain and posted to the 1st Battalion Depot in Burnham Camp as a company second-in-command. Here I got to know most of the new infantry subalterns who were training at the depot before being posted to Singapore. This was now a peacetime posting as New Zealand no longer had any troops serving in Vietnam. They were an interesting group – somewhat overconfident and cocky but I made sure the exercises I ran for them were sufficiently testing to challenge some of those traits.

Soon after returning to New Zealand I was sent on a lieutenant-to-captain promotion course for several weeks in Waiouru, which was not particularly enjoyable although I easily passed. Surprisingly, one of the instructors was one of my own former OCS classmates who up to this point had had exactly the same military experience as I had. I was highly embarrassed when the course leader failed my Fijian friend from NSTU days, the future prime minister of Fiji, Steve Rambuka, an excellent officer, from the Fijian Armed Forces, yet passed a New Zealand Legal Corps officer, who was pleasant enough but a military and tactical nightmare. It was incidents like these that caused me to lose a little faith in the traditional hierarchy of the army.

Our darling daughter Juliette was born on 15 September 1972 and, regarding home life, things could not have been better. But in terms of my military career I was getting increasingly itchy feet. I decided to apply for the New Zealand Special Air Service selection course in Auckland. I was dissuaded by my commanding officer at the time who informed me that I would have to pay for my own move to Auckland – an entirely inaccurate piece of information. But, in a way, it was the best thing he could have done because it forced me to look for another challenge elsewhere.

One of the company commanders in the 1st Battalion Depot was Huia W, who was an ex-New Zealand SAS soldier and an ex-British Army education officer with 22 SAS before he returned to New Zealand. He could see I was dissatisfied and persuaded me to follow my dreams. I wrote to then Brigadier Mike Walsh,

DSO (later Major General Walsh CB, CBE, DSO) who had been the brigade commander of 28th Commonwealth Brigade, which included 1 RNZIR, in Singapore from 1971–72. I had met him a few times after we had both returned from Vietnam. He advised me to contact the regimental colonel at the headquarters of the famed Parachute Regiment in Aldershot. This was Colonel John 'Joe' Starling, MC. I received a very positive reply from him; he was, I can confirm after later meeting him in person, a true gentleman. However, Colonel Starling informed me that I could only formally apply to join the Paras once I had resigned from the New Zealand Army to avoid any accusations of 'poaching'. Never one to shy away from risk, I did exactly this. Cecilia and I moved in with her parents and I got a job as a builder's labourer.

One of my jobs at the building site was to light a fire at 6am using off-cuts of timber in a 44-gallon drum so that the proper builders could warm their hands before starting work in the bitter, icy Canterbury mornings. I would go to work in my army boots and wearing green denims. One of the other workmen asked me if I had been in the military. When I said I had he asked me what rank I had been, 'A captain,' I replied. 'Jeez,' he said, 'What did you do wrong?!'

One of my other duties was to clean out the general latrine area (thankfully not the contents themselves), but this just reminded me of my days as a new recruit in the army, so I simply knuckled down and got on with it. We stayed with Cecilia's generous parents for some three months and each day I would get home from the building site and enquire if a letter had arrived from the British Army. For the first month I asked Cecilia to show me the letter as soon as I got back from work. At the start of the second month I asked her to come at lunch-time with the letter. In the third month I told her to come straight to work with the letter! Eventually, after three long months I received an official letter from the headquarters of the Parachute Regiment offering me a commission in the Paras – which I swiftly accepted.

3

3RD BATTALION, THE PARACHUTE REGIMENT, 1973-76

JOINING THE BRITISH ARMY

We received travel warrants and, with our baby daughter, flew via Singapore and then by VC-10 to RAF Brize Norton in the United Kingdom. I was posted to 3rd Battalion in Aldershot much to my great excitement!

On our arrival in the UK we were met by a Parachute Regiment corporal in a Land Rover. As we drove towards the army base in Aldershot we saw road signs warning about deer and we looked at each other and giggled – we were finally in England!

Our army quarter was in a housing area in Keogh Close which was opposite the Royal Army Medical Corps barracks near Mytchett in Aldershot. Our new home was a lovely two-storey stone house. We were used to New Zealand Army housing which was a plain wooden bungalow with only the very basic utilities such as an electric stove and a wood 'chippie' (small wood-burning stove) fire in the kitchen. Curtains and carpets were either brought from a previous house or purchased from the departing house occupant. This house was fully furnished including cutlery, crockery and everything else. We were very impressed by what the British Army provided for its officers in comparison. We couldn't be happier and I felt incredibly proud finally to be a member of the famed Parachute Regiment.

Regimental headquarters, or more likely the RAF (affectionately known as 'crabs'), wanted me to do a complete parachute course. The basic para course was about six weeks long. As a fully qualified paratrooper I wasn't too happy about this and I managed to convince the 'powers that be' to allow me to 're-qualify' after doing four balloon jumps – two by day and two by night onto Hankley Common near Aldershot. These balloon jumps were to be followed by a number of jumps from a C-130 Hercules.

Jumping from a tethered barrage balloon is a very unsettling experience. This massive beast, which in its former life had been a World War II barrage balloon, was winched up to 800 feet. The parachutists and the RAF dispatcher stood in a wicker basket suspended beneath the balloon. There were four 'jumpers' in the cage, as it was called, and a small gap in the side of the basket across which was a singularly inappropriate-looking skinny metal bar. The jumpers naturally pressed themselves into each corner of the cage desperately trying not to look over the side. The wind whistled through the balloon rigging lines making an eerie sound and this was complemented by the fearless and totally sadistic RAF parachute jump instructor (PJI) whistling happy tunes as he strolled about the tiny space remaining in the middle of the cage floor. Once the balloon had reached jumping height of 800 feet the PJI asked the jumpers to whistle a tune. This was a pointless exercise as each parachutist's mouth was completely dry! He then became very formal and ordered number one jumper forward. The PJI would then remind all jumpers that a green light in an aircraft and a command in a balloon were both military orders and must be obeyed.

The jumper moved to the basket entrance, the PJI lifted the bar and said loudly, 'Red on; Green on: Go!' On this command the jumper launched himself into the abyss shouting at the top of his voice, 'One thousand – two thousand – three thousand. Check.' He then thrust his head up to see if his canopy had deployed correctly. This was rather difficult as the World War II parachuting helmets and, later, the new ballistic helmets, were held forward by the parachute rigging lines as the parachute deployed, particularly if the parachute had twists.

Meanwhile, his companions, almost frozen with fear and quite ashen-faced, proceeded to carry out the same procedure under the orders of the PJI.

Following my balloon jumps I then had to complete a couple of jumps from a Hercules. In those days the RAF had 'stream training' which meant the aircraft would fly at low level for several hours, at about 200 feet, and then pop up just before we jumped out. This was to defeat the Soviets' radar. I can still remember the look on another Para's face when I asked him to remind me of the exit drills from a Herc! He did not want to be anywhere near me when we exited. Each plane carried only a few Paras and the flights were mainly to give the pilots practice in formation and nap-of-the-earth or contour flying.

It was a bit unnerving as the flights were very low and very turbulent and if you peered out of the plane's little portholes you could see that the hills were above the aircraft. In those early jumps I still have no idea where I boarded these aircraft or where I jumped out – I suspect I emplaned at RAF Lyneham and jumped out over Salisbury Plain. But all that mattered was that they gave me the tick in the box and so I was now accepted as a fully fledged 3rd Battalion, Parachute Regiment officer.

On arriving in the Parachute Regiment I was given the rank of lieutenant even though I was a captain in the New Zealand Army. So, soon after arriving, I was required to attend a promotion course which was a practical course over several days. I did the course at Mynley Manor which is a lovely old manor house in Hampshire then used by the Royal Engineers. Part of the course was to give operational orders and I was highly confident in doing what was required. I remember the officer running the course saying, 'You have obviously done this for real!' I felt rather proud to hear him say that.

I was posted to D (Patrol) Company where my officer commanding was Major Chris K; he would later win a DSO in the Falklands War. But much to my horror he sent me on a three-week unit accounts course at the Royal Army Pay Corps (RAPC) Centre at Worthy Down. Interestingly, this camp had been a Royal

Flying Corps airstrip in World War I. However, to me, that was the most fascinating part of the entire course. I had spent my entire commissioned life in the New Zealand Army avoiding such courses. The instructors were wily senior warrant officers and I was given delicately phrased encouragement at various stages of the course such as, 'Do you know what your problem is, Sir? You can't fucking well count!' and, 'Do you know, Sir, nobody has failed this course yet and you are not going to be the fucking first!'

Cecilia and I thoroughly enjoyed battalion mess life but there was one early toe-curling embarrassment when I turned up to our first curry luncheon in the colonial de-rigueur outfit of shorts and long socks. I was mercilessly ridiculed. A slight adjustment to my colonial background was quickly required.

Overall, I found the British Army officers more relaxed than their New Zealand Army colleagues. In New Zealand it was expected that a captain would salute a major and address him as 'Sir' and a lieutenant colonel was always as addressed as 'Sir' and never as 'colonel'. In New Zealand, status amongst officers was greatly valued and grudges were frequently maintained. In the British Army there was a much more relaxed relationship between the officers, and Christian names were used quite frequently. I believe this was mainly to do with the size of the British Army; in the New Zealand Army, which is tiny in comparison, the attitude of individual officers could adversely impact upon the entire career of a more junior officer. Moreover, in the British Army, although there was a gulf between officers and other ranks (OR), ORs were more forgiving of the inadequacies or immaturity of young officers, and NCOs could be relied upon to play a part in the forming of a good officer.

3 Para was my benchmark for the Parachute Regiment. I found the officers, especially the company commanders, very professional and old school. They were proud to be company commanders of Parachute Regiment soldiers – 'every man an emperor'. In later years, the ranks of the Parachute Regiment officers were increasingly filled with what I called 'thrusters' who were using the regiment as a stepping stone to stardom. I much preferred the old school version.

There was Gentleman Malcolm 'Bertson' C; Brian 'The Beast' W –
a nightmare at mess rugby; Geoffrey C who had wonderful stories
about his time as a defence attaché in Paris and who only drank
Campari and soda; Edward G who was a freefall guru; quiet but
forceful Graham F; John PW, another gentleman, but one who would
fall asleep during his own 'orders' group, much to the consternation
of those present (he suffered from narcolepsy); and Pat C. I was
privileged to serve amongst such illustrious company.

After the RAPC course I was sent on a combat survival course
held by the SAS in Hereford. Talk about the sublime to the
ridiculous – the courses could not have been more different! This
course formed part of the SAS selection continuation training for
their own members, but NATO pilots and Para Patrol Company
personnel could also attend. The course, designed to prepare
personnel who may become trapped in enemy territory, had
two phases – the first was 'combat survival' and the second was
'resistance to interrogation training'. The course was primarily run
in the Hereford area. The final exercise was held over a barren,
godforsaken part of North Wales.

Each course had a 'hunter force' which tried to capture the
'runners', us, as we made our way through the Welsh hills. On my
course the hunter force was provided by my own battalion, 3 Para,
and they were undoubtedly very keen to catch me.

I was grouped with Captain John A, a Royal Engineer from
9 Para Squadron and a combined services rugby representative, and
also a Para Brigade Education Corps officer (a 'schoolie'), although
I wasn't sure why the 'schoolie' needed to be on the course. In the
pre-escape 'strip-search' we managed to hide some tights about our
persons. We were driven to the escape area, around Lake Vyrnwy
in bleak North Wales and were dropped off in our threes, not
the normal pairs, because of the extremely bad weather. We were
wearing battle dress trousers and jacket; no shirt; boots with no
laces or socks; a greatcoat; and carried a bottle and tin each. We
jumped out of the truck as ordered and raced off the road into the
rugged hillside to get as far away from the road as possible and to
avoid the 'hunter force' which would be already looking for us.

The rain was pouring down and there was an icy bitter wind. The wind-chill was soon starting to affect us as we tramped over the hills following a bearing on our escape 'button' compass. We put the tights on our heads to try to minimise our bodies' heat loss. At one stage we looked at each other and fell onto the wet tussock laughing, almost hysterically. We looked like three giant rabbits with long droopy ears from the 'legs' of the tights. We appeared ridiculous as we stumbled along, each clutching our precious tin and bottle, and wondered about the reaction of a Welsh farmer if he suddenly came across these three giant rabbits with long ears in the mist and darkness on the Welsh moors.

The escape phase of this course involved moving across country to a final rendezvous (RV) as if we were escaped prisoners of war. We had to call in at checkpoints en route where we would be given a stale loaf of bread and the location of the next RV. At each RV would be an individual in civilian clothes and we would have to exchange passwords before we obtained any food or information. Prior to entering each RV, we would carry out a reconnaissance to ensure that hunter force personnel were not in the vicinity. We would then watch the RV until the designated time to enter it, with only one person approaching the RV.

Unfortunately, our 'schoolie' not only got one of the RV days wrong but went straight up to a military Land Rover and gave the password! Immediately, the Paras tumbled out of the vehicle and gave chase. The 'schoolie' ran straight towards our hiding place. John A jumped up to escape, lost his glasses and promptly ran into a tree and was put in the 'bag' as was the 'schoolie'. I ran as fast as I could away from the area. As I was running I heard footsteps running hard behind me and I readied for a fight to resist capture. I leapt over a fence and briefly turned around to see another 'runner' trying to get away as well. He had inadvertently been caught up in our melee.

Once we had both got our breath back we decided to move together. By now it was dark, and I was very hungry, so I went into a farmer's barn and found a bag of what I thought were sheep nuts for winter sheep feeding. I started eating them but half way through my second handful I had a sudden fit of panic – could they be rat poison pellets? I quickly dropped my trousers to obtain my 'escape capsule' which was concealed in my rectum. In this capsule was a candle and matches. I quickly lit the candle and to my relief discovered that what I had been eating was indeed sheep food. Yum!

We now had to make our way to an RV to the south of Lake Vyrnwy. The RV was on the other side of a small bridge through a town; this was an obvious choke point for the hunter force to be waiting. We managed to avoid their patrols and carried on into the countryside on the other side of the town. We found an old collapsed stone shepherd's hut to hide in and managed to light a small fire to try to dry ourselves a little. We also took the opportunity to brew some nettle tea and cook some rabbit that we had caught.

My new friend and I then cautiously left the hut and headed towards the area of the final RV. We found a huge Dutch (open-sided) barn nearby in which we could hide. I dug my way right into the middle of the straw and hid there. Interestingly, I heard the hunter force's dogs sniff all around the barn, but they did not find me. I don't know exactly where my new friend hid but he wasn't discovered either so at nightfall we met up again. We went to the RV where there was a large cattle truck waiting in the darkness. By this stage we were completely immersed in the full exercise scenario and really felt like fugitives!

We slowly crept up to the cab of the truck. I had a big stick with a nail at the end. My friend knocked on the driver's door while I waited by the passenger door thinking that if there was any aggression it would come from the passenger. The door opened, and I presented my stick with the nail but the driver and escort quickly identified themselves as the genuine article. They opened the little side door of the cattle truck and we climbed in and tucked ourselves into the piles of straw lying on the floor. Other runners began to join us in the back of the truck. These were mainly SAS aspirants including Cedric D and Arthur D, who both went on to become generals. The truck set off several hours later and we took the opportunity to try to sleep while we were being driven as we didn't know where we were going.

But it was a set-up! The truck took us straight to a disused Army training area in the SAS Pontrilas training area. The holding pens were in old World War II ammunition bunkers. A few years later these would be replaced by a bespoke, state-of-the-art complex.

The truck stopped, and we could hear low voices outside. The little side door opened, and a deep and threatening voice said, 'First one, oot!' We were now sitting up in the truck covered in bits of straw and all looking apprehensive. We looked at each other and somebody climbed slowly out through the door. We heard sounds of a short scuffle and then silence. Back in the truck I looked at the others and indicated that I was going to try to make a break for it through the cordon. Arthur D tried to dissuade me, saying that we would all be beaten up but my mind was made up. The scary voice now said, 'Next!' I moved to the door, put my fingers on the outside, and hurled myself out. Big mistake! There was a ring of grim-looking Paras outside the door and they merely extended the ring as I sat there growling and snarling like a Tasmanian devil. The result was very brief. The Paras simply closed in and enthusiastically overwhelmed me. I was dragged firmly into the cold, draughty concrete bunker, blindfolded, searched and made to lean on my fingertips, at an angle, against the wall for many hours.

I heard others being dragged in. I could sense Para guards moving silently amongst us. If I moved my hands or tried to stand upright firm hands would push me back into the leaning position. It is surprising how the smallest dimples in a concrete wall can become like needles on the ends of fingers after several hours. Occasionally, I would be forced down into a sitting cross-legged position with my hands on the top of my head. This made the muscles in my arms burn with pain and any dropping arms would be firmly and forcefully replaced on my head. After about six hours I was made to sit down and given a piece of dry bread and some water. My blindfold remained on, but I was able to glimpse other prisoners sitting or leaning on the walls around me.

I had heard scuffling noises and soon it was my turn as I was dragged off to a tent for my interrogation. The guards stood behind me and I was forced to sit on a low, one-legged stool. My blindfold was removed and, blinking in the light of a lamp focused on my face, I could discern a uniformed officer sitting behind a desk. I was asked who I was and I proceeded to say the appropriate mantra of number, rank, name and date of birth with which we had been trained to respond. As I became more and more tired and hungry this was a very effective mantra to repeat. Whenever I was asked for additional information I would simply say, 'I cannot answer that question, Sir.' This went on for some time and the interrogators would change around so that one was 'Mr Nice' and one was 'Mr Nasty'. All the while I was trying to maintain my dignity and stay upright on the wobbly one-legged stool.

Suddenly, Mr Nasty leapt to his feet while shouting abuse at me. Unfortunately, his foot must have caught in the power cord and we were all plunged into darkness. Mayhem prevailed! I jumped up and tried to find the entrance to the tent we were in, Mr Nasty was shouting at the sentry to catch me, and the sentry was trying to find me in the darkness. I managed to get out of the tent and was clambering up a chain-link fence when reinforcements arrived, pulled me down by my legs and I was bundled back into the pen and put up against the wall again.

I had not had my British Army regimental number for long and so, as the isolation periods dragged on I started to worry that I might forget it or jumble up the numbers confusing it with my New Zealand Army number. This would have immediately brought me to the attention of the interrogators – which was not something I wanted.

The interrogators would try to elicit a 'nod' or 'shake' of the head or obtain a signature on an apparently insignificant document. These could later be used in a totally different context for propaganda purposes. The hours dragged slowly and painfully. Although there was no physical violence we were now being entertained by 'white sound'. This is noise which has no rhythm, just abrasive ever-changing sounds. It can be compared to the static on a badly tuned radio. It is impossible to ignore and can become rather stressful. The white sound, blindfolds, isolation, lack of sleep and food took its toll on a number of candidates, who requested to be withdrawn from the exercise.

After several other interrogation sessions and some 36 hours I was finally taken out of the pen, my blindfold was removed, and I was told by someone in uniform wearing a white armband that the interrogation exercise was now finished for me. I refused to believe what I was told and continued with the mantra of number, rank, name and date of birth. Finally, I was persuaded that he was indeed a member of the directing staff (DS) and that my interrogation phase was actually complete. I received a very good grading on this course. It was undoubtedly an excellent learning experience and gave me a real insight into my mental boundaries and limitations which has been useful throughout my life.

NORTHERN IRELAND TOUR, 1974

3 Para was warned off for a Tour of Duty in Belfast, Northern Ireland in early 1974, and the battalion started its lengthy pre-Northern Ireland training. This involved numerous briefings and lectures about the Irish Republican Army (IRA) and the 'Troubles'. The term 'Troubles' intrigued me; it was a typical British Army understatement. The 'Troubles' started in August 1969 and were not technically concluded until 1 August 2007. They resulted in the deaths of 656 British soldiers and over 300 Royal Ulster Constabulary (RUC) policemen. The police and military deaths in the Troubles were more than those of the Falklands (255), Operation *Telic* in Iraq (179) and Afghanistan (456) wars combined. Some troubles!

The battalion was to be deployed to Belfast and would be based in the Flax Street Mill, which was located, unsurprisingly, in Flax Street, between the staunchly pro-IRA Ardoyne Road and the strongly Protestant Shankill Road. The battalion had been deployed to the Flax Street Mill on a previous tour so a number of the more senior officers and NCOs were familiar with the area. As part of this pre-Northern Ireland training, the battalion was deployed to the range camps at Hythe and Lydd. These ranges had been in use since the Napoleonic times. As well as the shooting ranges there was a bespoke training facility called Rype Village. This was an impressive complex which included streets and houses built to look like Northern Ireland as well as indoor areas with pop-up targets. In these indoor ranges the 'Toms' (Parachute Regiment soldiers) patrolled day and night, using a .22 Heckler and Koch insert in their 7.62 SLRs. Wooden targets would appear in windows and doorways, but not all of them were hostile and they could include women and children. This was to reinforce the strict rules of engagement (RoE) for Northern Ireland, and every soldier and officer had a copy of his Yellow Card with full details of when and where he was permitted to open fire. It was very prescriptive and was designed to avoid casualties amongst innocent civilians.

There were also a number of normal outdoor ranges where shooting competitions were held. I won the 7.62 SLR shooting competition and still have my bronze medallion. Hythe and Lydd was a very quaint coastal area with pebbly beaches and grey seas. We were training in late November and conditions were cold and wet. Fitness training involved long marches or 'tabs'; speed marches; and painful runs across the pebbles and boulders on the local beaches. Rype Village also had a 'tin city' which represented a typical NI security force base inside a small village complex. Companies and their platoons would be based here and patrol into the surrounding streets in four-man patrols or 'bricks'. The inhabitants of the village were provided from other units. Riots would be organised and included the use of stones, bricks and firebombs being thrown at troops as well as much verbal abuse. The 'villagers' entered into these riots with great enthusiasm, and this was responded to in kind by the Paras. These events had to be fairly tightly controlled to ensure that no major injuries were caused to either side. The training programme was controlled and managed by a military organisation called the Northern Ireland Training and Advisory Team (NITAT). This organisation prepared units due to depart on a four-month tour. Some units were deployed to the rural areas of

South Armagh, but most were based in the main towns and cities hence the significance of the training. The NITAT team had the task of confirming or otherwise if a unit was 'cleared' for service in Northern Ireland. This gave them quite a bit of power – something they seemed to revel in. It was worth more than a CO's career if his battalion did not satisfactorily complete its NITAT course.

It was extremely cold in the south of England and bitter winds swept through the training areas. To my embarrassment, I developed a huge, red infected nose which I assumed was something to do with the weather. The Patrol Company Toms were rather amused by my bulbous red 'shonk'. I remember Roger J, one of the company SNCOs, finding the matter particularly amusing. It was only many years later, back in New Zealand, that I found out that the infection was caused by toxin poisoning as a result of my service in Vietnam which had only been 18 months before I joined 3 Para.

Patrol Company's tasks in Northern Ireland would be patrolling in open Land Rovers and establishing covert observation posts in areas of interest. The Land Rovers had an angle-iron in the centre, which stood above the passengers and was bent forward at the top. This was a crude but effective method of defeating wires stretched across the road to behead any of the vehicle's passengers. The rifle companies had protected Land Rovers covered in Makrolon polycarbonate armour, which could defeat a low-velocity bullet and some high-velocity rounds. They had a hatch in the roof from which one of the patrol would observe to the rear of the vehicle. This protection would also assist against improvised explosive devices (IED) or nail bombs. The battalion also had old Humber armoured APCs called 'pigs'. This is about as simple an armoured vehicle as one can get. A basic truck chassis with a six-cylinder, five-speed manual transmission, 4x4, and seating for half a dozen or more with armoured protection on top of that. This vehicle was no speed demon. It was carrying a lot of extra weight so steering and braking were events that had to be given some thought. There were also the more modern Saracen APCs. This vehicle could carry, besides the driver and commander, a squad of nine soldiers. Most models carried a small turret on the

roof and there were ports on the sides through which troops could
fire. When the Toms deployed to areas of rioting they would wave
their red berets out of these rifle ports to let the population know
'the Paras are coming!'

The normal dress on patrol was the red beret with the Para badge
painted black and Vietnam-era body armour worn beneath the
distinctive camouflaged Denison Para smock. The Denison smock
had been worn by the Parachute Regiment in all theatres during
and since World War II. It was eventually replaced in the late 1970s
by a Para smock in normal disruptive pattern material (DPM),
much to the despair of Paras everywhere. The primary weapon was
the 7.62 SLR, and one end of the rifle sling was attached to the butt
of the rifle, with the other end attached to the holder's wrist. This
was to prevent the weapon being snatched away in a melee. Steel
airborne helmets were available if required. We enjoyed the fact that
we looked different to the rest of the army, the 'crap-hats', with our
red beret or distinctive airborne steel helmet and our classic Para
smocks. Mind you that did not endear us to our military colleagues
or to the army hierarchy.

Each patrol would carry one or two rubber bullet guns which
fired a non-lethal, black rubber bullet-shaped projectile. This was
known as a 'Derry dildo' or a 'rubber dick' by soldiers throughout
Northern Ireland. It was surprising how many disappeared into
the Ulster female community after they had been fired during
an incident. There was also a more solid plastic round. This
plastic round could not be fired without permission from a unit's
headquarters as they could be lethal. Each patrol had a radio, which
was either simplex or duplex. The simplex radios worked one-to-
one, whereas the duplex radios went via a rebroadcast transmitter
on a high feature in the area.

After Christmas at home, I deployed with the advance party
to go to Belfast on 20 February 1974. This involved a long road
journey from Aldershot to the docks at Liverpool to join the Royal
Fleet Auxiliary *Sir Galahad*. Tragically 48 soldiers and crewmen
would be killed on the *Sir Galahad* during the Falklands War, just
eight years later, when it was attacked by Argentinian Skyhawks.

After a cold, but uneventful night in a shared cabin I woke early to see the port of Belfast appear out of the gloom. The day was grey and grim and so was the port. We linked up with our escort from the 1st Battalion, Argyll and Sutherland Highlanders, loaded rifles and set off for Flax Street. The journey was very much an anti-climax after the hype of our pre-tour training. I looked at all the street names, now familiar thanks to my rigorous Northern Ireland training sessions. The streets looked normal except for the large concrete caisson roadblocks and some areas of bomb damage. We turned into Flax Street and almost immediately into the gateways of a tall, square red brick mill building to be greeted by 'Muttley the dog', the mascot of Flax Street Mill.

Beside the mill, surrounded by a high barbed wire-topped wall, was a large vehicle park in which were parked numbers of Land Rovers, Humber 'pigs' and Saracen APCs. But to my surprise, around the outside of the mill were normal houses, some of which overlooked the base area. This was not my only surprise. Over half of the mill was still functional but with entry for the workers through a different gate.

The handover programme involved being briefed by the intelligence staff of the Argyll and Sutherland Highlanders and then carrying out combined patrols around our new 'patch'.

The Ardoyne was virtually a ghetto with sullen residents, many blocked-up, empty houses, bomb-damaged shops, and several grubby corrugated-tin drinking clubs. The Shankill looked more normal, slightly, and the people were not openly hostile but cautiously friendly. It also had its share of empty bricked-up houses and seedy-looking drinking establishments. The unoccupied houses were bricked up to stop them being used by terrorists from either side as shooting positions. We also patrolled into Belfast city centre with its myriad of roadblocks and one-way streets. Here the scale of bomb damage was much more apparent. Armed patrols moved amongst the shoppers and business people, drifting into cover from doorway to doorway but being completely ignored by the public. The Northern Irish police, the Royal Ulster Constabulary (RUC) manned the various pedestrian checkpoints supported by

armed soldiers. At its peak the RUC had around 8,500 officers
with a further 4,500 who were members of the RUC Reserve.
During the Troubles, 319 members of the RUC were killed and
almost 9,000 injured in paramilitary assassinations or attacks,
mostly by the Provisional IRA. By 1983, this made the RUC the
most dangerous police force in the world in which to serve. As part
of the peace process it was eventually renamed the Police Service of
Northern Ireland (PSNI).

To my great disappointment I was advised that I was to be a
watchkeeper at the battalion tactical headquarters. This was
co-located with the RUC in the Tennant Street police station. The
company commanding officer, Chris K, was to be the battalion
operations officer or 'Kestrel' in military-speak. He was quickly
nicknamed 'Budgie' by Patrol Company soon after. As well as
being a watchkeeper, my job was to manage the company patrol
programmes and supervise the company administration matters
and, whenever possible, accompany the patrols. I could see this
was going to be a very long four months. Most of the battalion had
already served at least one tour in Northern Ireland and growing up
in the United Kingdom, they were very familiar with the situation
in Ulster.

My arrival in Northern Ireland was a great eye-opener for me.
I was particularly surprised by two things – the first was the low
key, almost defeatist attitude of many of the senior officers; and the
second was the almost casual acceptance of casualties received by the
security forces, even our own Para casualties. I have had experience
of serving in several national armies now and I do not believe any
other troops could behave in such a disciplined fashion over so
many years. As an example, on 27 August 1975, the IRA murdered
17 soldiers of 2 Para (including my friend Captain Peter F) in a
bombing at Warrenpoint in South Armagh. I was amazed that the
enraged Paras did not take the nearby town of Newry apart piece
by piece in a violent response.

The main body of the battalion arrived several days after my
advance party and soon settled into the task of 'maintaining an
acceptable level of violence' – this was the extraordinary stated

political task of soldiers in Northern Ireland! The facilities in the Flax Street Mill were very basic, but there was an SNCOs' mess as well as an officers' mess while the Toms had a canteen. There was also the resident char-wallah, who lived in two small rooms in the bowels of the mill. The char-wallahs, who were typically either Indian or Pakistani, maintained small kitchens from which they produced sweet tea, coffee and amazing 'egg-banjos'! No matter what time it was, day or night, the loyal char-wallah would be on hand with his beverages and 'butties'. These men were the unsung heroes of the war in Northern Ireland although they received little formal recognition and several unarmed char-wallahs were murdered by IRA gunmen in acts of pure spite.

Watchkeeping duties were certainly not my idea of soldiering and I resented the time I spent in the operations room. The room was on two levels with a clear plastic map board on which the locations of patrols and permanent observation posts (OPs) were marked. Hours were spent logging patrols in and out of the main base and the company sub-bases which were in separate locations from Flax Street Mill. The late-night shift – the 'graveyard' shift – received trays of sandwiches from the main battalion cookhouse. Unfortunately, by the time the control post (CP) staff received them they were completely stale and curled up at the edges. Nevertheless, after a long night watchkeeping we still enjoyed our 'smilies'.

Patrols, or 'bricks', always deployed in tandem so that each patrol could back up another and this also made it difficult for gunmen to ensure they had a clear exit route – their main requirement. Typically, a gunman would collect a weapon from a middleman/woman, who had obtained the weapon from a hidden cache. The gunman would engage his target, successfully or otherwise, leave the weapon and quickly make his escape ensuring that his hands and clothing were cleaned as soon as possible to remove any residue from the weapon's cordite. The weapon would then be collected by another stooge and concealed until next time.

Whenever a patrol entered the Ardoyne area the 'dickers', young children acting as lookouts for the IRA, would pass this information on to their handlers. Interestingly, the term is still used by UK troops in Afghanistan to describe children acting as lookouts for the enemy.

The street corners in the Ardoyne were painted white to show up patrols as they cautiously moved around the narrow streets. Individuals in a patrol would move from doorway to doorway to minimise their physical exposure and the last man in the brick would be watching the patrol's rear. We carried out a movement called 'ballooning' where you would constantly be moving your upper body as though you were a balloon in order to disrupt the target picture of a likely sniper. Yet we were all paid the princely sum of 50p per day 'danger money', which was, to be frank, somewhat of an insult.

The foot patrols I accompanied were mainly to carry out ID checks or personnel checks (P-checks) on the people in the streets. This information was radioed back to the battalion headquarters and the intelligence staff would check to see if any of the individuals were of interest. We would also carry out searches of the menfolk – these could be somewhat unpleasant due to a lack of personal hygiene. We could only search females if we were accompanied by a female MP or a female UDR soldier known as a Greenfinch. The Ulster Defence Regiment (UDR) was an infantry regiment of the British Army which began duties in 1970. Raised through public appeal, newspaper and television advertisements, its official role was the 'defence of life or property in Northern Ireland against armed attack or sabotage' but unlike troops from Great Britain it was not used for crowd control or riot duties. It consisted mostly of part-time volunteers until 1976 when a full-time cadre was added. Uniquely in the British Army the UDR was on continuous active service throughout its 22 years of service. In 1992, the UDR would be amalgamated with the Royal Irish Rangers to form the Royal Irish Regiment.

House searches were a real eye-opener for me. We would try to keep a balance between security of the area and intrusion. A house would only be targeted as a result of reliable information received. The house would be surrounded and a 'search team' would enter and carry out a thorough search of the premises. At the end of the search, the search team commander would have to obtain a signature from a member of the household confirming that no damage had been done. The majority of the houses were absolutely heaving and the search team members needed to have strong stomachs. Often, gross used personal items such as nappies, sanitary pads or even worse would be placed in drawers to conceal weapons or other items. Frequently there was also aggression from the occupants of the house as well as their neighbours. Paras do not frighten easily and the abuse given by the residents was mainly verbal. However, it usually did not take long for a very loud aggressive crowd to appear outside the house being searched. This was an incredibly threatening experience especially when we were grossly outnumbered.

At one stage of the tour I was in the Shankill Road on a patrol. The Shankill residents were not normally a threat but there was a confrontation with another Para patrol in a side street and a large mob had gathered and was attacking an armoured 'pig'. The mob had actually managed to rip off the driver's main door and attack him. How they tore off a steel door I have no idea. The patrol commander was a young Para officer. He was forced to open fire in self-defence and one of the mob was killed and several wounded. The word about the killing soon spread around the area. I was with a Patrol Company foot patrol in the Shankill Road accompanied by two open Land Rovers driving alongside us. Suddenly, the atmosphere turned very nasty and we were set upon.

It was like a football crowd suddenly appearing with the sole intention of lynching you. We withdrew towards the Land Rovers ready to quickly embus and drive away. However, one of the patrol sergeants, Alec C, fell, or was knocked down, and I have a clear image of a man raising a beer barrel to smash on his head. The whole issue of the Yellow Card had been drummed into our heads and, for a split second, I paused. I raised my rifle to shoot the man with the beer barrel. The sergeant then rolled away, quickly got to his feet, and jumped into the Land Rover. I jumped into mine and we rapidly left the area. My vehicle driver that day was Chris H, who like a number of Paras later joined 22 SAS, but sadly he was killed in Oman.

The battalion standing operating procedure at that time was for all the patrols, foot and vehicle, to immediately return to Flax Street in the event of a major incident. I personally thought that this was tactically unsound, and I wonder what would have happened if my patrol had been overwhelmed and all the other patrols had rushed back to Flax Street. It would have been too late to assist us. It was not the first time that I thought the battalion commanding officer was more concerned about not getting involved in dealing with the Irish and possibly getting a bad mark than looking after the safety of his own men. The Para officer was subsequently awarded the Queen's Gallantry Medal (QGM) for this action. He later left the army to command the Sultan of Oman's Parachute School.

Not all the patrols were as exciting as this and frequently the patrols would stop for a 'tea-stop' at a sympathetic Protestant individual's house. One or two patrol members would go into the house and chat with the occupants to collect information. I was a little naive back then and now I am quite sure that at least one of my senior sergeants – no names no pack drill – used his tea-stop as a 'bonk stop'.

At that time, there were two extremely popular TV programmes – *Top of the Pops* with the very attractive Pan's People dancers and *Star Trek*. It was very, very unusual to have any incidents when these two programmes were showing. This made me cynical about the real political intention of the gunmen if they could postpone their 'struggle' until their favourite TV programme was finished.

One of my colleagues in 3 Para was Dave C. He was training for SAS selection while we were in Belfast. He would train by running up and down the stairs in the Flax Street Mill with sandbags on his back! On our return to Aldershot he successfully passed the SAS selection course and was later posted to Hereford.

He subsequently served with 2 Para in the Falklands War and was awarded a Military Cross. He was quite a 'centurion' – that is, a very tough professional soldier. One of his quaint signs of 'endearment' was to walk up and stick a wet finger in your ear. In later years, he commanded one of the Sultan of Oman's Special Force Regiments as a contract officer.

I was certainly learning that the Paras, the Toms and the junior NCOs, in particular, were an unconventional lot and I always had to keep my wits about me. I recall being called into the city centre because of a bomb warning. We deployed in a cordon in the vicinity of the suspect vehicle. My Toms were taking cover generally in doorways of shops. I then took particular note of what sort of shops these were. The soldiers were hiding in the doorways of jewellers and the high-value shops but not in the doorways of Woolworth's or standard grocery shops. I have to say I smiled to myself – they were incorrigible. The bomb was eventually safely defused by an ammunition technical officer (ATO) so I did not have to carry out any personal searches of my soldiers before we returned to the Mill.

Towards the end of the tour, while on a vehicle patrol near the city centre, I received an urgent message to return to the Mill. My wife, Cecilia, had been taken seriously ill in Aldershot. The area around the city centre was a maze of dead-end streets which were blocked with concrete caissons and one-way streets. My drivers performed miracles, mostly involving some nifty pavement manoeuvres, to get me back as quickly as possible. It was a Sunday so there were no pedestrians about. Unfortunately, the end of the tall metal angle-irons on the Land Rovers went through all the shop front suspended lighting as we drove along the pavements. I was home in Aldershot within four hours.

Cecilia had had a brain aneurysm and had been taken to Cambridge Military Hospital and then to the Southampton Hospital neurological ward. Some kind neighbours had looked after little Juliette. I drove straight to Southampton to see her. Luckily there was no permanent damage, but it was a very frightening experience for both of us. I received compassionate leave and drove to Southampton each day to see her. Cecilia's mother was in England and so she came to look after Juliette and I returned to Northern Ireland to finish the tour. Cecilia was able to return home after spending several weeks in hospital.

The end of my tour in Belfast was a relief. Serving in Northern Ireland was an experience that I was not interested in repeating. The bigotry and the viciousness of both Protestants and Catholics were sickening to watch and this was underpinned by the zealots in the terrorist organisations which were all criminally based. The fear and the distrust of the civilian population were deliberately exacerbated by those who pretended to be seeking some moralistic outcome.

BRITISH ARMY EXERCISES

On returning to Aldershot, Patrol Company was heavily involved in a series of British Army exercises. On one of these the battalion deployed to Germany and Patrol Company was attached to the local infantry brigade headquarters as its reconnaissance asset. The company was based in a cow barn, complete with cows. The company HQ was located near the brigade HQ. I was most surprised to see how well the 'normal' Germany-based infantry officers lived on exercise in the field. They had full officers' mess facilities, complete with white tablecloths and regimental silver. We were all living in a wood and the other officers watched with some intrigue as I lived beside our command post under my Vietnam-era Australian poncho strung between two trees and cooked my meals on my hexamine cooker.

The next exercise was a parachute drop into the north of Italy as part of a battalion exercise with the Italian Army. Patrol Company was to fly straight from RAF Lyneham and jump on the first pass. It was a long flight and in a first for me we stacked our bergens and parachutes when we loaded onto the aircraft and after several hours on board we had a hot meal!

The conditions over the drop-zone were very marginal and there was quite a severe thunderstorm over the area. But a group of Italian VIPs were watching so clearly national pride was at stake – 'when in doubt get 'em out!' About 40 minutes out from the DZ we kitted up which was somewhat difficult as the aircraft was jumping around in the sky. We flew straight over the DZ and all exited on the first pass. We arrived just on dusk and as we were descending in the twilight there was the rumble of thunder and flashes of lightning all around us. It was exactly what I imagine a major operational jump would have been like in World War II.

Afterwards we were based in the Italian Ariete Armoured Brigade barracks at Aviano which were very smart. There were quite a number of Italian World War II armoured vehicles on plinths around the camp with details on the bases of great Italian armoured victories during the war – those were news to me. The Italian soldiers, mainly conscripts, lived rather well in their messes and the Toms were exceedingly pleased to see that wine was available with all meals. Also on the base were the Bersaglieri, a high-mobility light infantry unit. They can be easily recognised by the distinctive wide-brimmed hat decorated with black capercaillie feathers that they wear as part of their dress uniform. The feathers are also applied to their combat helmets. Each Bersaglieri unit had a band without percussion instruments called a *fanfara*, who played their instruments at the run while on parade.

We thought we looked rather smart in our red berets but in the fashion and musical stakes the quick-stepping feathered Bersaglieri had us beaten hands down!

We were involved in a number of joint exercises with the Italians and then we put on a major display of our equipment. The demonstration of the MILAN anti-tank weapon was somewhat interesting as on initial firing one of the control wires broke. The missile then started a journey of its own making, much to the concern of all the viewers, me included. Fortunately, it ran out of steam and fell out of the sky safely into the range impact area. The anti-tank platoon also featured on our return to the UK when we were going through customs at RAF Brize Norton. A few cunning old hands had concealed large containers of duty-free red wine in the barrels of their 106mm Wombat anti-tank guns. An alert

customs official spotted this and so we were all kept at the airport
for several hours while the customs officers pored over every inch of
our kit! But at least we had been able to do some sightseeing before
we left Italy. Most of the battalion visited Venice and I was amused
to spot several Toms cooking meals in doorways on their hexamine
stoves; Venice, after all, was and is an expensive city. The battalion
had some engineers from 9 Para Field Squadron, Royal Engineers
attached for this exercise. On their local leave they chose to go to a
taverna and start drinking. Not surprisingly they became somewhat
unmanageable in the evening after drinking a great deal of the
powerful Italian red wine. The taverna owner called the police. The
police in this case were the Carabinieri, who were not known for
their subtlety. A stand-off took place with the Carabinieri nervously
fingering their automatic weapons and the Para engineers standing
back to back holding the buckles of their web-belts in their fists.
The battalion RPs (Regimental Policemen) with the indomitable
Sergeant Paddy Brownlee managed to get between both parties and
defuse the situation. I don't think the engineers got a chance to see
much of Venice after that.

Historically, this part of Italy had been staunchly communist
since the end of World War II and the locals did not seem very
pleased to see us and so this incident did not help the cause of
NATO in the area.

I had done a military sport freefall course at Netheravon a few
weeks prior to this Italian exercise and took the opportunity to
carry out some jumps from the Army Air Corps Scout helicopter
that was attached to us for the exercise. I admit to not being a
very good or brave freefaller. Over the years I have done most air
sports – except gliding. I have a fixed-wing licence and I have flown
hang-gliders, paragliders and para-motors. As I said I've never been
a natural in the air and it is a love-hate relationship. In later years,
on a military adventure training exercise to Spain with the Services
Hang-gliding Centre I took off for my first major long-distance
flight and got caught by the wind and promptly flew straight back
into the mountain – I was soon back in the UK with a broken arm
from the crash.

I am obviously not alone in being a Para who didn't love all air sports. On my basic freefall course in Netheravon there was a Para major. I was a captain at the time. He later became a general. I don't think he enjoyed freefalling very much either. While parachuting in the local area we witnessed an RAF C-130 dispatching a parachutist who plummeted straight into the ground. We only found out days later that this was a dummy used for testing parachutes. The experience unsettled the whole course. I was surprised to see my Para colleague then withdraw himself from the jumping flight despite being manifested. Interestingly, he knew I had noticed and later at annual airborne forces cocktail parties he would make a conscious effort to ignore me. Funny that!

In early 1975 I went to the Jungle Warfare School (JWS) in Pulada, Johore Bahru, Malaya. I had spent some time there previously when I was in the New Zealand Army carrying out pre-Vietnam training. I was now attached to the current eight-week JWS course as an observer and also a participant. Later in the year 3 Para was going to carry out a six-week exercise and I was to coordinate the training. The JWS was run by an ancient infantry officer, Lieutenant Colonel Tony S, an eminent mountaineer. Unfortunately, he was a reactionary who insisted on continuing to teach tactics used by the Commonwealth troops during the Malayan Emergency when the opposition was small groups armed with World War II weaponry.

Our tactics for Vietnam had evolved so that patrolling was more aggressive and structured to enable our patrols to fight against a well-trained and well-armed enemy. I had a difficult time trying to convince this officer, for example, that circular harbours where troops would go into a circle in all-round defence at night had been superseded by the triangular harbour, which as the name implies, was in the shape of a triangle with a machine gun at each point. These machine guns could then effectively fire across the front of each part of the triangle. Sadly, this officer was a Luddite and I made

little progress in sharing my Vietnam jungle warfare experience
with him.

The course was based in *attap* (grass) roofed huts in a large
camp surrounded by numerous shooting ranges and tall *lallang*
grass. This grass was difficult to move through and in the tropical
heat it was like trying to move through a furnace. Once inside the
jungle canopy conditions improved. Generally primary jungle is
quite pleasant to operate in but the worst tropical environment is
secondary jungle which has grown up in an area where the primary
jungle has been cut down. This type of jungle is very thick and
difficult to penetrate.

There was another Para on the course from my battalion,
Lieutenant Roger 'Todge' W. We lived in the officers' mess at
HMS *Terror* naval base in Singapore, near the causeway to Malaya.
We would drive up to Pulada for the week's training and then
return to Singapore at the end of the week. In another nearby
camp, Nee Soon, was a British infantry battalion. At the end of a
lengthy Friday 'happy hour' in the Nee Soon officers' mess, Todge
needed to get back to HMS *Terror*. The only available vehicle he
could see was the battalion duty officer's Land Rover. Using his
airborne initiative (ABI), he decided to borrow the vehicle and
drove himself back to his billet. He was very thorough and made
sure that when he arrived he cleaned all his fingerprints off the
vehicle, using the handiest material available, which just happened
to be the duty officer's white mess kit jacket. Satisfied, he then
went into his room and to bed. All would have gone well, if he had
not parked the Land Rover outside his own room. The military
police soon located the Land Rover – and him! Paying for the
dry-cleaning of the duty officer's jacket was only one of his many
penalties. Todge later joined the Army Air Corps and became a
well-respected helicopter pilot.

After the course I returned to the UK for leave and then travelled
back to Singapore with the battalion advance party to prepare for
the battalion's arrival. The flight to Singapore was in an RAF C-130
Hercules which was stuffed full with equipment and people. One of
the Toms spent the entire journey sleeping in one of the adventure

training kayaks strapped to the top of a vast pile of stores. His 'bed' was much more comfortable than the extremely uncomfortable C-130's webbing seats.

The journey was interminable. We landed at nearly every one of the RAF staging bases then in use – Akrotiri in Cyprus, Masirah off Oman, Gan in the Maldives and eventually, four days later, we finally arrived into Singapore. A week later, the rest of the battalion arrived and, after several days of acclimatisation, started exercising in the jungle. The battalion was based mainly at the Jungle Warfare School with periods of leave back into Singapore. This was the first time that the Paras had been back in the jungle since the days of Borneo. In Borneo, Para patrol companies work alongside SAS units. One old hand in the battalion was Major John 'Patch' W. In 1965, as a young NCO, he had won a Distinguished Conduct Medal, when his actions had helped defeat a major assault by the Indonesian Army on his jungle base during the Malaya Confrontation. He lost his eye during the fighting and wore an eye-patch. Despite his having to endure several surgeries on his injured eye, his career went from strength to strength; he became the regimental sergeant major of 2 Para and was commissioned into 3 Para.

But, for the majority of the battalion, living and training in the jungle was a new experience. Once the Toms realised the jungle could really be your friend they adapted well and became very proficient. In true Para fashion they worked and trained hard, and then partied hard. It didn't take long for the men and officers to discover the infamous 'Boogie' Street in Singapore. On the roof of the public toilet building in the centre of the street the Paras performed many renditions of 'Zulu Warrior'. This is a classic Para Party trick in which naked or semi-naked individuals compete in trying to sing all the words to the song 'Zulu Warrior' before a burning length of toilet tissue, which is clenched in their bottom, reaches a critical part of their anatomy. These antics were observed by a happy, cheering mass of soldiers, sailors and airmen – and bemused locals. It was only when the military police intervened that trouble would begin. To a tipsy serviceman the red cap of an

MP is like a red rag to a bull. There was, however, little resistance when the local Singapore police arrived as they certainly did not mind breaking a few heads with their batons.

After six weeks the battalion returned to Aldershot, having survived Singapore and the jungles of Malaysia – and Singapore having survived 3 Para.

In late 1975, Patrol Company was sent down to South Armagh to carry out covert patrols along the border with Eire. This was before the SAS was formally deployed to Northern Ireland. We were based in Bessbrook Mill and loosely attached to the local battalion there – one of the foot guard regiments.

In the small officers' mess in the bowels of the mill this regiment had a great slab of Stilton cheese. Beside the cheese was a World War II US steel helmet and beside the helmet was a polite little printed note which said, 'In the event of a mortar attack, please place the helmet over the Stilton before retiring. Thank you.' Such panache!

We carried out recces, performed covert patrolling, established OPs and investigated suspicious buildings and farms along the border. We could operate quite independently because everyone at the time was so frightened of the IRA in South Armagh. We were able to operate much more freely than when I went back there with the SAS. We had more explosives and equipment than you could shake a stick at. I had claymores, grenades, explosives – all sorts of things tucked into the Bessbrook Mill lift shaft. We used Scout helicopters a lot and became very fond of them. We were almost always overloaded and on several occasions I came back, almost frozen, standing on the skids as we flew into the Bessbrook Mill LZ. Some flights in the mist were interesting to say the least.

One night found us patrolling along the main railway line which had been frequently sabotaged. We saw some figures acting suspiciously near the line and when challenged they ran away into a field near a haystack. We could not find them and as I thought they must have hidden in the haystack I fired a Verey pistol into it. It burned nicely but nobody appeared. I got some very funny looks from my patrol as we watched the haystack burning – I suspect this was not the way the British Army normally operated.

We also established a fixed OP on Slieve Gullion Mountain overlooking the town of Flurrybridge and the border crossing point at Forkhill. This OP dominated the local area and gave us excellent observation of the houses of local Forkhill suspects over the border in Eire. It also overlooked a well-known farm that straddled the border which was used to smuggle livestock and petrol back and forth across the border. Unfortunately, the IRA never challenged us on Slieve Gullion as we were well protected with American claymore mines and other surprises. That was the first and only time I saw the claymore in use here. It was replaced by a pathetic little device called a PAD – protective area device. Apparently, the claymore was far too aggressive for Northern Ireland!

The intelligence we had at the time was minimal and we were not able to establish a useful link with the local RUC or Special Branch. One of the locations we also observed was the local pub, The Three Steps Inn, in Drumintee. This was where British Army officer Bob N was kidnapped in 1979 and later murdered in the woods above Jonesborough near the Forkhill border crossing point into Eire. He was foolishly carrying out an unauthorised undercover visit to the pub and had no backup. At the time he was rumoured to be operating as a liaison officer between the SAS and Special Branch.

We were only in South Armagh for about six weeks, but we came to know the local area very well and this greatly assisted me when I deployed back to Bessbrook Mill with the SAS in 1977.

The Patrol Company sergeant major was 'Barnie' B (RIP) who was a great character. He always chewed gum and never hesitated to voice his views on military matters. He was a highly experienced Para and well worth listening to. He had done an attachment with the Rangers in the US and he used to upset them, not deliberately, by sleeping in the body bag they were all issued with. He said it was perfectly weatherproof and was an ideal bivvie-bag. There were some excellent NCOs and Toms in Patrol Company and I really enjoyed working with them. Names such as Ernie R, Dave F, Alec C, Manny M, Dickie B, Dave 'Blue' H, Mick Q, 'Blue' C, Lou S, Ian J, 'Digger' G and many others. The company performed well under fire in the Falklands and several members received serious gallantry awards – John P a Distinguished Conduct Medal (DCM), 'Beetle' B a Military Medal (MM), Des F an MM and Kiwi Rick A an MM (posthumous). I met many of them after I had left 3 Para and we still keep in touch.

After the company's spell on the border in Northern Ireland, I was posted from Patrol Company to take the appointment of battalion training officer.

I now worked in battalion headquarters, in the 'head-shed', and I had two senior NCOs to assist me – 'Gunny' Gonifas and Murray Smith. They were very experienced Paras but they both had a wicked sense of humour and I was frequently the subject of their mischief. They once rang the commanding officer, who was not known for having a sense of humour, and handed me the phone saying the CO wanted to speak to me. The CO and I then had a very confusing conversation as to who had rung whom. After I eventually hung up the phone, I noticed Gonifas and Smith choking with mirth at their desks across the office.

One of my first tasks as training officer was to organise and run a junior NCO course in Omdurman in Sudan. The battalion was due to be deployed to Sudan for a four-week exercise and to work with the Sudanese Army.

We were the first British troops to train in Sudan after its independence from the United Kingdom back in 1956. In 1972, the Sudanese government became more pro-Western and looked to the British Army for support and training.

We were based in an old, former British army camp in Omdurman, which was some 12 miles from the capital of Khartoum. I found it a fascinating country with a rich culture and a blend of the Arabic north and the African Christian south, which met in the melting pot of Khartoum and Omdurman. It was also, of course, an area rich in British military history. Here the battle of Omdurman had been fought in 1898 when the British, under the command of General Sir Herbert Kitchener, defeated the army of Abdullah al-Taashi, the successor to the self-proclaimed Mahdi, Muhammad Ahmad. It was a demonstration of the superiority of a highly disciplined army equipped with modern rifles, machine guns and artillery over a vastly larger force armed with older weapons, and marked the success of British efforts to re-conquer the Sudan. There had also been a famous charge by the 21st Lancers, 400 strong, who had attacked against a force approximately 2,500 strong. Four Victoria Crosses were subsequently awarded. I was pleased to discover that there was still a well-maintained memorial to the 21st Lancers near to our camp which I visited as well as some other battlefield sites.

The training area was hot, red stony desert, interspersed with small hills and *wadis* (gullies) and covered in sparse thorny bushes. On exercises in the surrounding desert we would pass long camel trains and once we came across a small well in the middle of a desert area and there was a Bedouin family, complete with goats and donkeys, filling up their goat skins and jerry cans.

We did a parachute jump with the Sudanese troops. We were told they were para trained, but I had my suspicions as I watched them hanging in their harnesses, grinning broadly as they descended to thump onto the desert floor. Their camouflage uniforms did not fit and they wore no socks with their boots. Their equipment was all from Soviet sources including their weapons and armoured vehicles. We had a combined sporting event with the Sudanese soldiers and they completely outclassed us on the cross-country but the battalion redeemed itself in the boxing ring.

Visiting the *souk* or market in Omdurman was a fascinating experience. It was filled with local produce in baskets sold by smiling, squatting women in their colourful garb. A lot of the menfolk were tall Arabs with extraordinarily large white turbans and long gowns or dishdashes. They walked in ornately covered leather sandals. The Sudanese Arabs have a reputation as teachers and in later years I would meet them throughout the Middle East. They were always well educated, well spoken and very polite. While I was wandering around the souk, several Sudanese came up to me and said, in perfect English, 'Welcome to my country'. In Khartoum itself was the anachronistic Khartoum Club. This was a walled, colonial haven where the expats would congregate for tiffin and then nightly cocktails. It was a pleasant location, complete with a shaded swimming pool, ballroom and magnificent library.

I even visited the former governor's palace on the banks of the Blue Nile. Famously it was on the steps of this palace where General Charles Gordon of Khartoum met his death in 1885.

There were very few places for the soldiers to go for in-country leave between exercises so someone arranged for two- or three-day breaks to somewhere called Dum Dum Island on the Blue Nile. This island was opposite Khartoum and was reached by a very old-fashioned Nile steamer. The soldiers allowed on leave would take ration packs, beer and their tents and pile on to the steamer. Dum Dum Island was sandy and blisteringly hot with little shade. A stay there was almost a punishment. The Toms joked there was a raffle organised in which the first prize was two weeks on Dum Dum Island and the second prize was three weeks on Dum Dum Island. There were few, if any, facilities on the island, but it did ensure that the mean soldiery was kept well away from the expat community in Khartoum. The CO was always worried in case there was an incident which would not reflect well on his personal confidential report and so Dum Dum Island was the ideal answer for him.

I recall being woken one night during my spell on Dum Dum by a low singing. I looked out from under my pup tent to see a long line of buck-naked Paras walking through the sand on their knees singing the song from *Snow White and the Seven Dwarfs* – 'Hi Ho, Hi Ho, it's off to work we go!' They all had a can of beer in one hand and a piece of wood over their shoulders. I watched transfixed as this column made its drunken, happy way from one end of the small island to the other. It has to be one of the funniest sights I have ever seen.

One of the field training exercises I ran for NCOs was a realistic grenade range. Most grenade ranges in the UK are very formal concrete blockhouses from which grenades are thrown over thick blast walls. Soldiers are nervous of grenades, understandably, but if realistic training is managed properly this fear is replaced by confidence. In this case, the NCO students would lie behind small bunds dug into the sand and throw their grenade, observe where it landed, and then lie down behind the mound until it exploded. All was going well until one young NCO, who had decided to put masking tape around the handle of his grenade to stop it being accidentally detonated, threw his grenade forgetting to remove the tape before he pulled out the pin. The grenade did not detonate because the lever was held in by the tape. Contrary to normal practice I decided to recover the grenade so that we could carry on with our training rather than carry out a long-winded demolition process. But the heat of the sun and the sand were slowly melting the adhesive of the masking tape and the grenade lever was slowly moving away from the grenade. As I moved towards the grenade sitting malevolently in the sand I knew I had seven seconds before it would explode once the lever flew off. I could run a long way in seven seconds. I picked up the grenade, removed the tape, threw it into the desert and took cover. Bang! – job done.

When we had finished our exercises in Sudan we moved to Khartoum airport to meet the RAF C-130s which were to return us to the UK. We were sitting on the black tarmac, roasting in the sun, awaiting the imminent arrival of the 'crabs'. We waited and waited until we were finally informed that our aircraft had been 30 minutes away from Khartoum when it developed a minor fault, so it turned around and flew some three hours back to Cyprus. There was obviously no way that the precious RAF crews were going to spend the night in hot, sweaty Sudan. We moved off the runway into the very basic airport building to spend a miserable hungry, thirsty and mosquito-besieged night. Ah well – if it ain't paining then it ain't training! We finally left the following day.

Back in the UK, the training team and I would also run NCO courses in the Otterburn training area in the north-east of the country on the border between England and Scotland. This was a wild, open expanse of hilly rolling country covered in tussock grass. The area seemed to attract the worst weather and in winter was covered in snow. It was also the home to a vast army of midges and sandflies! Running through the centre of the area was a well-preserved Roman road joining the remnants of several legion camps. It was easy to imagine columns of Roman legions trudging along this road to and from conflicts with the wild, woad-covered Celts in the north just as we trudged along the same routes.

In Otterburn, Gonifas and Smith continued to keep me on my toes. On one particular day, as one of the NCO courses was practising fire and movement with live ammunition, I was on a hill overlooking the range. I was firing over the heads of the soldiers so that they could experience the distinctive 'crack' and 'thump' of incoming small arms fire. Suddenly, Gonifas grasped his head and fell to the ground. I thought I had shot him and I was about to race down to minister to him when he stood up, gave me a cheery wave, and carried on as if nothing had happened.

Back in the accommodation in Otterburn, in the summer months, Gonifas would have strings of meat drying on the fence lines. He was of South African extraction and this was his precious biltong being prepared. There were also a number of plump pheasants in the training area near our billets and several dressed birds appeared in the cookhouse. Apparently, some of the training team would go hunting at dusk, after training had been completed for the day, armed with a .22 calibre Heckler and Koch insert in their SLRs. An SLR 7.62mm bullet does not leave much of a pheasant whereas the .22 bullet does not substantially damage the birds. Moreover, the SLR looks quite normal in the event of a suspicious gamekeeper appearing. More airborne initiative!

After I had completed the combat survival course I had applied to attend an SAS selection course. I had liked what I had seen of the unit and so I wanted to see if I was good enough to join them. But the Parachute Regiment was good to me, so I delayed my application until I had been with them for three years. I was eventually advised that I could attend the SAS selection course running in February 1976. This would be a winter selection and one which I preferred to the summer selection course. The selection course was based in Hereford and run in the harsh country of the Brecon Beacons and the Black Mountains.

I had been training seriously around the lanes of Aldershot running in boots and with my webbing and bergen. My fitness target was to be able to complete the final 'endurance march' of 30 miles in 16 hours carrying personal webbing, rifle and a bergen weighing 60 pounds.

As part of the training in November 1975 I took a patrol from 3 Para on the Cambrian March, now known as the Cambrian Patrol. This exercise is considered one of most arduous and prestigious military events, testing candidates' leadership, field craft, discipline and both mental and physical robustness. Teams of eight were required to cover over 30 miles carrying an average of 66 pounds over unforgiving Welsh terrain in less than 48 hours. Patrols were also required to undertake a number of 'tasks' on their route, each testing a different aspect of soldiering such as map reading, first aid and casualty evacuation, recognition of aircraft, vehicles and equipment, a tactical river crossing, a speed march, and a shooting competition.

Each patrol task was set within the context of a narrative which involved teams having to traverse enemy territory and interact with friendly and not so friendly civilians or militia groups. Points were added or deducted depending on time and conduct while on the patrol. The Cambrian Patrol is still in existence, although it has evolved slightly to suit the requirements of modern soldiering. It is the closest thing to Special Forces selection many people will experience.

I am very proud to say my patrol won all the stages, with the exception of the shooting where we were pipped to the post by … I hate to say it … a Royal Marine patrol.

But I needed to train in the actual area where SAS selection was being held so I rode my 400cc Honda to Wales as often as I could. I stayed in the army barracks in Brecon and went off into the hills from there. The motorcycle journey was almost a selection course in itself, as the journey was so cold. I only wore my military clothing and, in those days, this was not very wind or waterproof. I would have to stop at many of the motorway service areas en route to try to defrost in the warm air from the hand-driers in the toilets. I was able to sharpen up my navigation skills in the rain and mist of the Beacons and made sure I knew my way around the dreaded Pen y Fan area. This steep Welsh mountain was to feature heavily in my selection course. Interestingly, it also had a Roman road running up to it from one side. Once again, I felt immense sympathy for those Roman legionnaires tramping along on those long, straight stone roads in the pissing rain of England, Scotland and Wales.

4

22 SPECIAL AIR SERVICE REGIMENT, 1976-80

SELECTION

Eventually the time came to travel to Hereford's Bradbury Lines, the home of 22 SAS, to start the SAS selection course. This course had a number of phases. There was an initial physical weeding out process where attendees had to complete the normal British Army fitness tests. Surprisingly, a few failed even these tests. Over the next few weeks we went to the Brecon Beacons and Black Mountain areas in groups and then in pairs. This was to ensure that those from other corps, not infantry, were sufficiently competent and fit to be able to operate alone in the area. These initial marches were part of the general fitness attrition of candidates. A number of those on the selection felt that they had to impress the SAS training staff who accompanied us into the hills by moving at a very fast rate which we all had to match. I knew that this was not wise because we were using up valuable energy before we even started the final and gruelling 'test week'.

I remember standing up in the back of a four-tonner that was taking us back to camp after one of these marches and reminding the others that we did not have to race each other and that what we were doing was not going to be helpful in the long run. I also recall a number of my fellow candidates looking at me with a certain amount of derision, clearly thinking that I was not able to keep up the pace. I passed several of them on Test Week lying beside the track completely drained of energy and unable to finish the course.

If a candidate had a bad day, he was given a 'gypsy's warning' that he needed to improve his timings. If the candidate failed to improve he was described as going to Platform 4. This was the SAS euphemism for 'Thanks for trying but now fuck off.' Platform 4 was the platform at Hereford railway station for the London-bound train.

The routine in the camp was very relaxed and although we ate centrally in the main mess hall we lived in our own respective messes. There was no pressure put on candidates to continue or to voluntarily leave the course. At the end of each day candidates were briefed on the activities for the following day and it was up to them to prepare themselves and be at the vehicles ready to depart early the next morning.

The final physical week of the course was Test Week, which involved daily individual treks across the valleys and mountains of Wales. At the start of each trek all candidates were given a grid reference (GR) and we made our way to that grid reference where we would meet a member of the SAS training staff who would then give us the next GR and so on. The treks became longer and longer each day and the weights we had to carry increased. One of the treks was euphemistically called 'Fan Dance' and involved going to the top of Pen y Fan from three sides. On another trek Ordnance Survey maps were replaced by hand-drawn 'escape' maps. Despite the weather or the terrain candidates had to travel at a minimum of 3 kilometres per hour!

·I had two aids during these long tiring treks. One was a small plastic cup on the end of a piece of para cord tied to my smock. This cup was actually one of Juliette's and was embossed with baby animals. It allowed me to scoop up water from streams to drink as I raced along and it meant I did not have to open or refill water bottles. The other aid was a small portable radio and earphones so that I could listen to music as I ploughed through the snowdrifts. I particularly remember at 11am each week day listening to Dave

Lee Travis and his 'Tiny Tots Session'. My favourite song and one which drove me along was 'We got us a convoy!' by C.W. McCall. I now always smile when I hear this particular song. I never knew whether the SAS staff would think I wasn't taking selection seriously by having a radio so I always hid it whenever I approached a selection RV.

The final hurdle was 'endurance'. This was the long 16-hour trek across approximately 37 miles of the Beacons. The twist in the tail was that you did not know when you had reached the final RV. More than a few candidates gave up when they received a new grid reference to walk to when they were expecting to have reached the final check point. As a touch of cruelty, the final RV and waiting four-tonner were sometimes only 200 yards around a corner from the penultimate RV. It must have been heart-breaking to give up and then realise that you only needed to walk another few yards to the finish line.

I successfully completed Test Week and then, as an officer, I also had to survive Officers' Week. Officers' Week had a physical component but naturally included a requirement to carry out operational planning for various SAS-type operations. These plans were then presented to an audience of SAS officers and senior NCOs who would thoroughly challenge them. Their questioning was very robust and even if they personally agreed with the plan presented they wanted to establish how a very tired and nervous young officer would act under pressure. Once again, on a day-to-day basis there was no pressure or even assistance from the training staff. You were given a task at any hour of the day or night and it was up to you to sort it out.

There were two other remaining officers, including a fellow Parachute Regiment officer, on my course and I watched them cheat during Officers' Week by walking along roads during one of the cross-country treks. Using roads was forbidden; if you wanted to take the risk it should only be done at night, but these two were ambling along roads in broad daylight. Using roads was obviously a great deal easier than navigating and moving across the unforgiving terrain of the area. They both failed selection but to my surprise they were both permitted to stay on in Hereford and attend the next selection, which they failed yet again!

My selection course had started with ten officers and 100 soldiers but in the end only ten soldiers and I passed.

JOINING 8 TROOP

After the initial selection course candidates were required to complete some months of Special Forces skills training culminating in a 'resistance to interrogation' course and parachute training. As I had already completed the latter two, I attended a six-week junior staff course at the Infantry Centre in Warminster. After that I was finally able to officially join 8 Troop, 'The Lions of Mirbat', B Squadron of 22 SAS in mid-1976.

The other troop commanders were Cedric D and John M. Cedric D had been posted to B Squadron from another squadron; he was a very intelligent but taciturn, insular man who tended to communicate by grunts and mumbles. John M was a Para engineer officer who was abrasive and singularly overconfident. He would later serve as a squadron commander for B Squadron. During the Falklands War he made it obvious that he was very unhappy with a planned operation for his squadron and so he was unceremoniously 'sacked' by Peter de la Billière, the Director Special Forces at the time. In an interview I had with Peter de la Billière some years after the Falklands War he described John M's actions as inexcusable! John M and I were to meet again later in the Sultan of Oman's Special Forces.

8 Troop, B Squadron's mobility troop, was composed of a number of experienced SAS soldiers who had served several tours in Oman. An 8 Troop patrol had been a key element in the success of the British Army Training Team (BATT) and the local Omani gendarmerie in defeating the attack by a large group of 250–300 communist-trained insurgents on the town of Mirbat, a provincial capital. The troop commander, Captain Mike K, was awarded a Distinguished Service Order (DSO) – an unusually high gallantry decoration for a captain's rank; Sekoi 'Take it Easy' T (also known

as 'Tak') was awarded a Distinguished Conduct Medal (DCM), and another Fijian, Talaiasi L (known as 'Laba Laba'), was awarded a posthumous Mentioned in Dispatches. The attack took place on 19 July 1972. There was a team of nine SAS operatives in a local house, supporting a small number of Omani soldiers who were based in the old Mirbat fort.

Tragically, prior to taking command of an SAS squadron, Mike K died of exposure in the Brecon Beacons while joining a selection course in extremely adverse weather. After he died Cecilia and I would see Arthur D, a fellow troop commander who was a great friend of Mike and his wife Maggie, visiting Maggie. Years later they were married, which was a happy ending to a very sad event. Some years later, as second-in-command of the Sultan's Special Force, I had the pleasure of escorting Arthur and Maggie around the fort at Mirbat when they visited Oman. She was finally able to see where Mike and his troop had fought so gallantly.

But all this was still in the future. For now, I was extremely honoured to take Mike's place as troop commander, although he was a tough act to follow. B Squadron was mainly composed of fellow members of the Parachute Regiment and had a reputation for operational aggression even within the SAS Regiment. Most members of the SAS are free-thinkers, but B Squadron and 8 Troop seemed to have more than most. I was glad that I had had operational experience in Vietnam and this certainly helped me become accepted by the troop.

8 Troop had many characters within its ranks and all with a wicked sense of humour. Throughout my three and half years with the troop this sense of humour prevailed, no matter what the operational circumstances were or the level of danger. I don't think I have laughed so much with any other military organisation I have been with. Don't get me wrong, they were exceptionally professional and took their Special Forces soldiering very, very seriously but they would always be ready with an amusing cryptic comment or observation on events that were happening.

Kevin 'The Airborne Wart' W was one of my troop sergeants. He was also a Para and a short, gobby Londoner, and very funny. When the troop was carrying out motorcycle training on its old BSA 250cc plodders in the Hereford city area we came to a red traffic light. Unfortunately, Kevin was really rather short and when he went to put his feet on the ground having stopped at the light he fell right over. The hot exhaust pipe then lay across his leg and he protested mightily. The rest of the troop could hardly stand up as they were so convulsed with laughter. He was eventually rescued by John W, another of my troop sergeants, before too much damage was done. John W was a calm Scotsman, the image of the dour Scotsman in the old TV series *Dad's Army*. John's brother had been killed by the Indonesians while serving with the SAS during the Borneo conflict. I was fortunate to have John to calm down some of my exuberant ideas – he was a thoroughly good man. The third sergeant in my troop was 'Gentleman' Jim V. Jim had been awarded a Military Medal in a battle at the Shirashiti caves near the Yemeni border where he was wounded in the leg. He and his fellow Fijian, Laba Laba, had been very good friends. Jim confided in me one day that as B Squadron was flying into Salalah airfield over Mirbat to start an operational tour, Laba Laba had leant over to Jim, pointed to Mirbat below the C-130 and said, 'I am going to die there'. I could not have asked for a better team of men.

One evening, before going into town, Kevin W turned up in the sergeants' mess in Hereford in a very smart, brand-new, Mao suit with a high collar. Kevin fancied himself as a ladies' man and he did seem to have a following amongst the Hereford ladies although it may have been pure curiosity on their part. At about 3am the Ministry of Defence Police, called the 'Mod Plod', were patrolling the camp area when they observed a large object entangled in the barbed wire atop the fence surrounding the sergeants' mess. They stopped to investigate and there hanging upside down 'like a bat' was Kevin, completely entangled in the wire in his new suit and 'three sheets to the wind'. It seems that he had returned from town and had mislaid his access card for the mess gate and so had decided to climb the fence before becoming entangled. Kevin was part of a 22 SAS team which tested the fences and walls of government establishments and he had an amazing reputation for clearing most obstacles at great speed. However, in this instance, a number of pints of Hereford's best ale and his unfamiliar Mao suit conspired against Kevin's clearing the fence that night.

'Sailor' (also known as 'Snapper') W was another colourful character in the troop. He had also been at Mirbat – manning the .50 calibre heavy machine gun. He was a very competent Special Forces operator, but he did not always have the best of luck. He was sent on an SAS team task to Hong Kong to work with their Special Duties Unit. He was looking forward to the task but one night he was invited to join some Hong Kong Special Branch officers for a social evening. Some trouble started in a bar and the Special Branch officers left 'Sailor' on his own as he was being assaulted by a group of men. Naturally, he defended himself but unfortunately, when the regular Hong Kong police arrived and detained everyone involved, they found a knuckle-duster on 'Sailor'. The laws against carrying 'weapons' in Hong Kong were very, very strict and 'Sailor' was found guilty and given an option of six months imprisonment or four 'strokes of the cane'. He chose the cane which turned out to be a huge bamboo pole wielded by the one of the biggest men he had ever seen. Sailor described the pain of the beating as simply horrendous. He returned to the UK after a short stay in the military hospital in Hong Kong – on his stomach – and was RTU'ed (returned to unit) on his return. Before he left we were playing rugby for the unit against a local team and Sailor, as he was changing into his rugby strip, showed me the vicious wounds from the caning and said, 'I am the only sergeant in the British Army with four stripes – and they are all on my fucking arse!' After having completed two years or so of 'penance', he would return to Hereford, complete SAS selection again and finally re-join B Squadron. He continued to have a successful Special Forces career, featuring prominently in the SAS termination of the siege at Princes Gate in London and in the Falklands War.

Taking command of an SAS Troop was quite a daunting prospect for an officer new to the SAS. Each squadron in 22 SAS treated its new officers differently. There was a very influential core of senior NCOs within 22 SAS and they could make life difficult for a new officer. Two new troop commanders arrived after the routine departure of Cedric D and John M once their tours as troop commanders had finished. Both new officers were from the Parachute Regiment. One of these fellow troop commanders, a fit Para, was nicknamed Captain Trigger, a TV personality of the time. His fitness got him through selection, but he was not accepted very easily by his own troop. His troop sergeant made Trigger's life very difficult.

The other troop commander was Mike 'Rough House' R. He had joined the army later than his peers. He was a solid, no-nonsense officer but had a tendency to be overly serious and was prone to over analysing every situation. He had taken over the post of second-in-command of 3 Para Patrol Company when I had left the Parachute Regiment and our paths seemed to keep crossing. He gained his nickname when B Squadron took over the UK Counterterrorism (CT) role. When the CT teams were on standby or between periods of training they entertained themselves, and kept fit, by playing 'murder basketball'. This was a no-holds-barred game with the basic, and I mean very basic, aim of getting a medicine ball (a large, heavy leather-bound item of gym equipment) from one end of a hall, room or field to the other. It was an all-ranks affair and many a perceived slight was rectified during the melee. It wasn't long before a local rule had to be introduced which was that each 'player' had to have a boxing glove on one hand. This was to try to lessen the physical damage to persons and bodies. 'Rough House' participated fully and played with extreme vigour and probably a little too much aggression.

The answer to this enthusiasm was for both sides to pass him the ball and then both sides would proceed to maul him. I am not sure to this day if he realised that he was always being set up and that that is how his nickname originated.

DEPLOYMENT TO NORTHERN IRELAND

In January 1976 Prime Minister Harold Wilson announced that the SAS would be deployed to Northern Ireland, and an element was based in Bessbrook Mill in South Armagh. We were deployed towards the end of 1976 to replace the original squadron. We were also based in Bessbrook Mill. Of course, I had been in Bessbrook Mill with 3 Para Patrol Company the previous year and so knew the area reasonably well. We were to carry out OPs with the aim of apprehending armed members of the IRA.

Most of the squadron's operational experience had been obtained, for a few, in Borneo and, for the majority, on tours in Oman. Very few of the old hands had served in Northern Ireland. Whenever I grew tired of hearing war stories about Oman I would make a disparaging comment about 'that police action' and reinforce the fact that Vietnam, where I had gained my operational experience, was a 'real war'. This would always lead to robust discussions about the merits of each conflict.

We travelled to South Armagh with the Royal Marines from, I believe, 45 Commando. This commando was replacing 3 Para as the battalion in residence in the area. On our arrival I met quite a few members of Patrol Company, my old company, who reminded me with great amusement that I had said I would not be coming back to Northern Ireland when I left to go to the SAS!

South Armagh was known as 'bandit country' and a number of British soldiers had been murdered there. The physical area is small with few roads and lanes. Patrolling soldiers could only use so many different ways to get from point A to point B. The IRA, from their safe sanctuary in Eire, could lay mines or booby-traps knowing that someday a soldier would stand on them or set them off.

We became adept at establishing and maintaining rural OPs, spending days watching the homes of local suspects in an attempt to photograph them with weapons or explosives. This photographic evidence was necessary in the laborious legal follow-up in the event that we killed an armed terrorist. On a lighter note, as it was a mainly rural area, we would often find that cows, as curious creatures, would take a great interest in the bushes in which we had set up an OP during the night. This was a dead give-away to any farmer that someone was on his land. We bought a number of catapults with which we would fire stones at the cows as they peered into our 'homes'. I still have my little camouflage-painted plastic catapult.

We carried out a certain amount of vehicle surveillance but carrying out mobile surveillance in a rural environment can be somewhat tricky. There is little other traffic and the locals are very aware of any new events happening. We used to say that the farmers counted the sparrows on the telephone lines each morning. A particularly challenging operation was to follow and 'house' a person of interest who was on a tractor! We needed at least eight vehicles and even then I suspect we were 'pinged'.

On another task, we were carrying out a vehicle 'follow' when we were caught up in a mob of sheep in a country lane. I was next to the farmer as we stopped and tried to negotiate our way through the sheep. In my best Ulster accent I said, 'How are you, now?' but after the third exchange of similar pleasantries he was obviously well aware that we were not from 'round these parts'!

It was initially difficult to get the older troop members to learn the need for silence when patrolling or in an OP. Their previous operational experience in the wide-open spaces of the Middle East meant that they had to get used to talking, cooking and eating silently. If we wanted to get a tactical advantage over any IRA who were skulking about the area to set up landmines, attack the homes and families of UDR men and women or snipe at army patrols we had to be quiet. It took a few weeks of me having frequently to go 'Shush!' to eventually get the message across. I remember standing up in one OP and banging some mess tins together to emphasise my point – we quickly vacated the OP that night.

There was not a great deal of 'good' intelligence for us to work on and one of the reasons for this was that the Northern Ireland military hierarchy was very nervous about our presence in the province. They seemed to be convinced that SAS soldiers would be totally uncontrolled and would cause mayhem and murder. In line with this we all had to have our personal weapons forensically tested before we arrived in Ulster to ensure that all our weapons had a recorded barrel 'signature'. Ridiculous and quite unnecessary measures like this certainly did not endear Headquarters Northern Ireland to us at all. Moreover, we were not permitted to establish direct links with the RUC Special Branch officers. These policemen knew more about their own 'patch' than anyone else and they had continuity whereas British Army units came and went. In order to communicate with Special Branch we had to operate through appointed non-SAS army liaison officers (LO). These LOs were of mixed ability and more than one was an SAS 'wannabe'.

The IRA had started setting up illegal vehicle checkpoints (IVCP) in the areas close to the border with Eire where military vehicle patrols were few and far between due to the risk of roadside IEDs. If we received information that there were IVCPs being set up in the local area we would cruise that area wearing civilian clothes in nondescript civilian cars with the hope of coming across one of these road blocks. We were very heavily armed on these patrols with M16 rifles, Heckler and Koch MP5 sub-machine guns and my preferred weapon of choice – the M79 grenade launcher.

We did not achieve a great deal during this tour in terms of military successes, but we gained valuable experience in working in a rural environment close to the border with Eire and we certainly did succeed in restricting the movement of the local IRA.

COUNTERTERRORISM ROLE

One of the main attractions of the SAS for me was the diversity of tasks that we carried out. When we came back from Northern Ireland, I took over command of one of the two UK counterterrorism (CT) teams. The teams were called Alpha Team and Bravo Team. This was a four-month task and we were on 15 minutes' standby throughout that period. We had to be able to send an advance team to any part of the UK in the shortest possible time, by vehicles, aircraft, boats, parachutes, or a combination of these.

We spent a great deal of time training and shooting in the 'killing house' throughout the duration of our CT role, continuously practising our drills. The 'killing house' itself was a purpose-built shooting range inside a building in which various situations and scenarios could be prepared. We only used full-bore ammunition in this building so accuracy and safety were absolutely essential.

But before 8 Troop and I even took over responsibility for the UK CT response we were mentored by the team in post from another squadron. This was serious stuff because if they did not give us the 'tick' of approval we would not be able to take over the role. During the lead-up training we were in the 'killing house' about to make an aggressive entry into one of the rooms where there was a hostage and terrorists (in this instance wooden targets only). I was the assault team commander and number two in the line-up while number one had the shotgun to blow off the locks on the door. On our radios I counted down, 'Standby; standby – go!' At this command number one shot the locks off the door, moved aside, and I rushed forward, pumped full of adrenalin, and attacked the door pushing it with my full might. It would not open! I thought this was a 'special' – introduced by our trainers specifically to test me and so I attacked the door with even greater aggression. But it would not move. The rest of the team with their MP5s and stun grenades was closed right up behind me ready to enter and clear the room. Then ... one of the trainers leant over and whispered in the ear of my gas mask ... 'Boss, it's a "pull" door!' I took a while to live that one down. But otherwise training progressed smoothly, and we successfully rotated onto CT duty.

As the team commander I also had to spend a lot of time giving lectures to all sorts of dignitaries and VIPs, including members of the Royal Family, who came to visit Hereford. Often, we would take them into the killing house and they would play the role of a 'hostage' in a terrorist situation. They would be with an SAS chaperone and would sit on chairs with three or four 'terrorist' wooden targets around them. At a given signal the lights would fail, and the CT team would burst into the room preceded by several 'flash bang' grenades with their deafening bangs and blinding flashes. There would be bursts of automatic fire and the hostages would be unceremoniously dragged out of the room. Then the lights would be turned on and the disorientated and flushed hostages would be shown around the room that they had just left. The preceding sequence of events would be explained to them. Most of them thought it was jolly exciting until they realised that the CT team had been using live ammunition as indicated by the closely grouped bullet holes in the targets that had been right beside them.

———

Throughout our CT role we travelled in white Range Rovers, often ten in a convoy. It was an impressive sight as we raced down motorways at speeds of over 110 miles per hour. We were always preceded by a Hereford traffic police car with sirens and flashing lights, and we had blue lights on our vehicles as well. As we reached each police district we would be met by a police liveried car from the district we were entering which would then travel with us to the next police boundary. On one call-out we were going to transit a small rural police area. Waiting to escort us at the county line was a little police panda car – I don't think that car ever saw us again.

One of the main routes from Hereford to the south of the UK was across the older Severn Bridge which connects Herefordshire and south Wales. It had toll booths at the English end and as we sped past I remember seeing the toll booth attendant pressed against the far wall of his booth with his mouth wide open as we hurtled through the narrow gap.

Often on a rural run we would have a helicopter above us advising us if the route ahead was clear to overtake civilian vehicles. We had to smile at the looks of absolute horror on the faces of civilian drivers as we overtook them in 'unusual' places.

Our driver training was carried out by two brothers from the Herefordshire police and they would take us out in our Range Rovers and teach us how to drive safely at incredibly high speeds. They were excellent and instilled in all of us a real confidence in our own abilities as well as teaching us how to read all the features of a road. They would sit calmly in the passenger seat telling each driver to go faster and faster – much to the horror of the driver and more so of the other SAS members in the rear of the vehicle awaiting their turn.

We trained and trained but during my time we only had one genuine call-out, which resolved itself without our intervention. Just four years later, in 1980, B Squadron would be called upon during Operation *Nimrod*, for the famous Iranian Embassy Siege and the rest, as they say, is history. I was proud to know that 8 Troop was at the forefront of the action that day.

———

Towards the end of 1977 I attended a surveillance course in London run by one of the security services. It was an excellent course and the trainers were very good. However, because they were normally working in a benign environment some of the techniques we were taught would not be successful in an environment where there was a hostile third party, as in Northern Ireland. This is an environment where the general public is hostile and information on any unusual activity would be passed directly to members of the 'target' community.

Following this course, I worked with Major Julian 'Tony' B training selected military people for serving with 14th Intelligence Detachment or the 'Det'. This was a volunteer undercover surveillance unit specifically designed for operation in Northern Ireland from 1973. The aim was to create highly trained, highly skilled undercover, plain clothes surveillance operatives. It was open to all members of the armed forces (and later, highly unusually for a Special Forces unit, women were allowed to apply). Operatives came from all ranks of the military and the Special Boat Squadron (SBS). The Unit's officers for NI operations were selected from suitable commissioned candidates.

'Tony', other selected SAS personnel and I ran a rigorous physical and psychological selection course for candidates at a secret camp in the Midlands and then continued the training in another training area. This training involved foot and vehicle surveillance, the accurate use of firearms carried covertly, advanced and aggressive driving, navigation, the use of 'hides' both rural and urban and photography. The selection and training was comprehensive as the operatives would be working alone in an extremely hostile environment where even a small mistake would lead to a 'compromise' and could get them killed. I went on a couple of visits to Northern Ireland to visit and operate with the 'Det' teams to ensure that our selection and training remained appropriate. Subsequently when the SAS was deployed to Northern Ireland we would work closely with the 'Det'. They would carry out what they were really good at – surveillance – and we would carry out any 'executive' action that their surveillance necessitated. This was to ensure that the 'Det' operatives always maintained their anonymity. There was a certain amount of relatively good-natured rivalry between the two organisations. They called us 'The Hooligans' and we called them 'The Walts' or 'Walter Mittys'. This friendly rivalry still continues between the Regiment and the 'Det's' modern offspring, the Special Reconnaissance Regiment.

Throughout the 1970s and '80s, the 'Det' was probably one of the most highly decorated organisations in the British Army but they also took a number of casualties. There was one individual we were training who was excellent in every way but as a left-hander in training ambush situations he often had trouble firing his handgun quickly from the car. The handgun was normally secreted under the right thigh while seated in a car. I was not happy for him to deploy and failed him on his course. I was overrruled and regretfully he was later shot and killed during an IRA vehicle hijack situation.

During my service with 22 SAS I was frequently away from my family for months at a time, but the CT team role meant that we remained based in Hereford, albeit at 15 minutes' notice to move and always carrying a pager. So, throughout this four-month tour I was able to spend time at home with Cecilia, Juliette and our brand-new son, Andrew.

After my CT tour I was fortunate to be included in an SAS officer team that attended a seminar planning the counterterrorism responses for the 1980 US Winter Olympics. Four of us attended: Maurice T, 'Spike' H, Terry H and me. We worked with FBI agents from all over the United States as well as Secret Service agents. I was always amused when Secret Service agents would give me their business cards and there plain as day was their name and 'Secret Service Agent'! We also worked with the US 'Blue Light' team from 5th Special Forces Group, a 'Delta Force' team and a team from the German Grenzschutzgruppe 9 der Bundespolizei (GSG 9) counterterrorism unit. GSG 9 had recently had experience in the aircraft hijack in Mogadishu which they had successfully concluded – with some assistance from Alastair M and Barry D, both from 22 SAS.

We had many interesting seminars comparing various tactical and shooting techniques as well as various methods of entry skills. There was more than a little testosterone flowing as each national and international group was keen to demonstrate its own particular expertise.

One lengthy discussion was about the best method of correctly selecting the right sort of man for a counterterrorism team – one who would be able to aggressively enter the enemy stronghold and be prepared to kill the terrorists and not freeze at a critical moment. The FBI agent running the seminar paused and looked at our group and asked, 'Well, how do you Brits manage this problem?' There was a slight pause and then our spokesman, Maurice T, in a rather over-laconic voice said, 'Well, up until now, we didn't know we had a problem.'

In late 1978 I was selected to take a four-man team to East Africa to train a presidential bodyguard. This was a task carried out on behalf of the British Foreign Office. My team members came from another squadron. They were Dave F, Vince M and Phil J. There was a long preparation required for the task as we needed to be totally self-sufficient including course materials, weapons, explosives and medical drugs.

It was a very challenging, but interesting task; however, once again, the SAS cover stories we were told to use were unconvincing, and it didn't take long for the local expat community to realise that we were not the simple 'builders' that we said we were. In fact, I remember being met at the airport on arrival by the First Secretary from the British High Commission who asked me how long the British Army had been employing mercenaries. I had no idea what he was talking about but apparently the Ministry of Defence was charging the Foreign Office for all our pay and allowances. I thought it was a bit out of order for him to give me a hard time about it.

The previous presidential bodyguard team had been trained by the North Koreans and we were the first Western unit to be working in the country since their independence. We lived in a house in the hills about 30 minutes outside the capital. The country was interesting but in a poor state of repair and the military ranges we used for shooting and demolitions training had not been maintained since the British had left in the 1960s. The presidential bodyguard was organised on tribal lines and the key personnel in the team were certainly not the most effective ones. I thought it was quite ironic that, here we were, training Africans in how to use Soviet weapons and teaching them British tactics.

At the end of the tour we were taken on a tour of the game parks by the president's office. We visited Arusha, the Ngorongoro Crater and Lake Manyara. It was an incredible experience. Many years later I was able to show Cecilia these amazing places too.

At the completion of this task we flew back to the UK by a commercial carrier and we were accompanied by a number of our stores and weapons that had been originally taken by an RAF C-130 Hercules. These items were in a diplomatic bag which travelled with us. On arrival at London Heathrow we went through the customs 'To Declare' channel. I duly declared to the HM Customs official on the desk that we were carrying both drugs and weapons. His face fell and after directing me to stay where I was he disappeared into the little spyroom that customs officials always have at airports. We could just glimpse lots of activity going on behind the glazed glass panels.

As we were waiting I casually observed the 'Nothing to Declare' channel and there was a brightly dressed Caribbean lady with a big bag on the counter with one large bottle of rum beside it. When I looked again there were three bottles; finally there were seven large bottles of rum beside her bag. She was looking distinctly crestfallen while the customs official was looking very triumphant. Meanwhile, in our channel a very self-important customs official came striding out to take over the situation. In a nutshell we had our personal phials of morphine which we carried around our necks and we had our personal 9mm Browning pistols – but no ammunition, as it had all been given to the host country. Eventually, after many phone calls and much discussion, we handed over the pistols and morphine which were then sent to Hereford police to be returned eventually to us. We got the pistols back, but we never saw the morphine again.

RETURN TO NORTHERN IRELAND, 1978

In December 1978 we returned to Northern Ireland based outside South Armagh. We lived in small portacabins and were ostensibly part of a Royal Signals organisation. We carried out undercover rural and urban patrols as well as foot and mobile surveillance. We were working in conjunction with the 'Det' once again, with the intention that we would be the 'executive arm' if any IRA locations were discovered. We carried out OP tasks and mobile surveillance in most areas of Northern Ireland except Londonderry, which was too small for us and the 'Det' to operate in together.

On one occasion we received information that the police station at Warrenpoint near Newry was going to be attacked by the IRA. To prepare for this operation I flew back to a small airfield in the UK to collect a number of 9mm Heckler and Koch MP5 sub-machine guns including two SDs – the suppressed versions. I flew back with Jim V in an Army Air Corps Auster. We had to wear full immersion suits because we were flying over the Irish Sea in a single-engine aircraft. The flight began in a startling fashion when the super keen Army Air Corps pilot took off too soon after a commercial Boeing 737. The turbulence from the wake of the jet in front of us nearly inverted the stocky Auster. I was pretty pale whereas Jim, a Fijian, was an interesting shade of grey. The flight was thankfully uneventful after that dramatic beginning. We collected the weapons and headed back to Belfast.

We had carried out a full recce of the area around the police station which was bounded by civilian houses and a playing field. We borrowed a dog from somewhere and casually walked around the area remembering to look the part and not arouse suspicion. On the evening of the proposed attack we made a covert entry onto the flat roof of the police station. I had about six members of the troop with me. Other members of the troop were parked close by in a covert van to act as a quick reaction force. We positioned ourselves so that we could see the surrounding area and we had already identified likely approach routes. The police station was unmanned at this time. At about 1am, we were using the Starlight Scope, a single lens, early type of Night Vision Goggle (NVG) – but better over long distances than the more modern bifocal NVGs. NVGs were optics that utilised all the ambient light at night to provide a green, relatively clear view of one's surroundings – like night binoculars. They were effective out to about 300 metres. Through this Starlight Scope we observed three to four figures approaching the police station from the playing field area. We repositioned ourselves to improve our fields of fire and awaited the approach of these individuals. As soon as we identified weapons we would challenge them. Unfortunately, we could not see any firearms or packages which could have been explosives, so I reluctantly withheld our gunfire. We remained in position throughout the night even though the visitors had left after about 30 minutes of studying the police station. It was clearly a reconnaissance mission prior to the actual attack. A few days later the individuals in question were arrested as part of a Special Branch operation.

On another operation we inserted an ambush in the driveway of the house of the General Officer Commanding (GOC), Northern Ireland. We had received information that his house on the outskirts of Belfast was to be attacked by an IRA active service unit. The local infantry battalion was the Black Watch and so we combined our ambush insertion with one of their routine patrols in the area. We were dressed in camouflage uniforms and heavily armed with M16s, MP5s and shotguns. The Black Watch patrol commander, a New Zealander called Dick P, decided to give me an update on what his patrols had or had not seen as he passed me in my ditch in the bushes. This was very helpful

My father and mother, just married, in 1940. My father was a battery sergeant major in the Royal Artillery deployed to France with the BEF and was withdrawn from the beaches of Dunkirk. He returned to France in June 1944 and, as a troop commander in a 17pdr Achilles tank destroyer with the 75th Anti-Tank Regiment, RA, 11th Armoured Division, fought through France, Holland and northern Germany.

Author (centre) at a forward airfield in the Cameron Highlands, Malaya watching the deployment of troops and supplies by Wessex helicopter during the Malayan Emergency in 1957.

Private MacKenzie newly qualified as a rifleman in the Royal New Zealand Infantry Regiment in 1966.

Equipment jump from an RNZAF C-47 Dakota (ParaDak) in 1969. Author is third from the rear on the starboard side.

NZ infantry (3 Platoon, Victor 5 Company), M60 gunners deployed in South Vietnam, 1970.

The author on operations in Vietnam.

Lieutenant Alastair MacKenzie being briefed by Lieutenant John Winton (KIA 10 March, 1971), South Vietnam, 1971.

Travelling on a Centurion tank in Vietnam.

Victor 5 Company deploying from M113 Armoured Personnel Carriers.

Patrol Company, 3 Para, 1974 – Para and child in Ardoyne, Belfast, 1974.

Patrol Company, 3 Para, 1974 – carrying out a 'P check' in Ardoyne, Belfast. 'Dickie' U provides 'top cover',

The author at Bessbrook Mill helipad, South Armagh, 1977.

Patrol Company, 3 Para, 1975, South Armagh. The 'Night Stalkers'.

FBI Academy, Quantico, USA. Briefing on tactical options by German Special Forces (GSG 9), 1978.

A Company, 1 Para, 1980. 'MacKenzie's Light Horse' patrolling the border between Hong Kong and China.

A Company, 1 Para, 1980. Showing VIPs around the border town of Sha Tau Kok.

44 Parachute Brigade, South African Defence Force, 1981. Carrying out Resistance to Interrogation training for the Brigade Pathfinder Company in the Caprivi Strip, South West Africa.

Brigade Pathfinder Company, 44 Parachute Brigade, South African Defence Force, 1981. In South West Africa, a fighting column of 'Jackals' and Unimogs deploy into Angola.

UNITA child guerrillas in Angola.

Remains of an RNZAF Sioux recce helicopter which crashed in 1984 in Waiouru, NZ while assisting on a Grade 2 Officers' Staff and Tactics Course. All three occupants were injured, one very seriously, and the helicopter started burning. The author was in the immediate vicinity and helped rescue the injured and provide first aid.

The author's final field exercise in the NZ Army as second in command of the 2/1 Battalion Royal New Zealand Infantry Regiment in 1985.

The Oman Counterterrorist Team, 'The Cobras', carrying out aircraft assault training in 1984.

The author receiving the Order of the Special Emblem from Sultan Qaboos bin Said of Oman. The author was second in command of the Sultan of Oman's Special Force and commander of the Oman Counterterrorist Team, the Cobras, 1985–88.

HQ of the Cobras, 1986.

The Cobras carrying out maritime CT training in the seas off Hong Kong on a 'ship underway' with the Royal Hong Kong Police Special Duties Unit.

The Cobras carrying out close quarter battle shooting with UK Special Forces.

SSF parachute training with equipment into Oman.

The author as a sales manager with Royal Ordnance (UK) in 1991 demonstrating the use of Explosive Cutting Tape© to destroy a German World War II aerial bomb at a military base somewhere in the depths of Finland.

Above Carrying out a maritime security survey in Trincomalee harbour and other national harbours on behalf of the Sri Lanka Government and Port Authority to assist in countering the threat of the 'Sea Tigers' arm of the Tamil Tigers.

Left Working in Phnom Penh, Cambodia with the UN mine disposal agency as part of a Royal Ordnance/British Aerospace project in 1992.

Below As an independent consultant observing a training aircraft assault being carried out by the Bulgarian CT Team, 'The Red Berets', at Sofia Airport in 1998.

Attending the first UN Military Observers Course held in Russia in February 1996. The course was held in midwinter at the Vystral Higher Military Academy near Moscow. When driver training in the inimitable Lada, four-wheel drive was only engaged when conditions were really difficult! At the time the author was a Territorial Army officer commanding a Brigade Specialist Training Team.

Left In 1999, the author, as a British Territorial Army officer and also a Vietnam veteran, was a 'speaker' on the first British battlefield tour of the wars in Vietnam, the first tour by any foreign country permitted by the Vietnam Government. These Vietnamese soldiers photographed at Dien Bien Phu would have been the grandsons of the North Vietnamese Army soldiers who the author fought against in 1970–71.

Left Crossing the USA on Route 66 from Boston to LA in 2014 with the Artists Rifles Motorcycle Club – what a great crew!

On return to NZ, in 2006, the Year of the NZ Veteran, the author organised a charity motorcycle tour of the whole country by all the Returned Servicemen's Associations in NZ on behalf of the Vietnam Veterans and their Children Trust. The riders finished at Parliament Buildings in Wellington. The other riders were Bruce G and 'JC', both NZ Vietnam veterans, 'Gizer', a serving NZ veteran, and the amazing Dave Barr, USMC Vietnam veteran and double amputee.

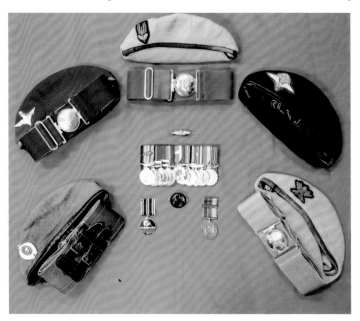

Clockwise from lower left: green beret of the Royal New Zealand Infantry Regiment and stable belt; Parachute Regiment beret and stable belt; SAS beret and stable belt; dark maroon beret of South African Parabats; imperial purple beret of the Sultan of Oman's Special Forces and stable belt. Centre: top: South African Parachute Wings, worn on chest; second row, left to right: Vietnam Medal General Service Medal with Mention-in-Dispatches (Oak-leaf); Vietnam Service Medal (NZ); Northern Ireland General Service Medal; Long Service Medal (NZ); Vietnamese Service Medal (S. Vietnam); Pro Patria Medal (South Africa); Southern Africa Operations Medal (South Africa); Order of Oman (Oman); Peace Medal (Oman); 15th Anniversary Medal (Oman); third row, left to right: Operational Service Medal (NZ); SSF Counterterrorist Team Clasp – Cobra (Oman); Military Service Medal (NZ).

of him, but I did have to ask him rather sharply to speak to his patrol and not to keep talking directly to 'my' bush. Early the following morning a vehicle pulled up at the end of the road we were watching, and several men got out. I thought, 'Here we go!' and we all tensed waiting for the group to get closer. Disappointment again – this little group was obviously using the driveway as a 'comfort stop' on the way home after a long night at the local pub.

We deployed OPs whenever we received good intelligence. We often used old vans which had no military links. A driver and a 'shotgun' would take out the OP team and they would carry out a rolling debus near their selected 'drop off' point. When a patrol had completed its task or needed resupply or the collection of exposed film a pair would move from the OP to a pre-designated spot and a van would carry out this task.

On one return trip we had a major scare when some drunks in a car threw a beer bottle against the side of the van and it exploded in a shower of glass. For a heart-stopping second we thought it was a grenade or a bomb and that we were under attack. We operated very successfully using these vans but there were still clear risks. In a subsequent SAS tour one covert patrol had the misfortune to debus in the middle of a group of IRA setting up an ambush just beside the border with Eire. There was a firefight and sadly Al S, from 7 Troop, was mortally wounded. He was awarded a posthumous Military Medal for his actions in this contact. After my tour with the SAS Al S had been my signals NCO with A Company, 1 Para before he went to Hereford. I knew him well.

Despite the conditions and the environment there were, as always, many humorous incidents during this particular tour. Due to the numbers of OPs we were conducting our complexions had become distinctly pale. One of my troop, 'Rusty' F, felt he needed a bit of a tan on his face. He obtained a small infra-red lamp and in his free moments he would work on topping up his tan. Unfortunately, one day he fell asleep in front of the lamp and his face became bright red with blisters. He now had a bright red face to match his nickname. He was mocked unmercifully and ended up doing even more time in OPs because he was unable to go on the streets as he was immediately recognisable.

In the camp we would all eat with the young signallers in the camp cookhouse. This cookhouse had certificates behind the serving point detailing who had won the 'Cook of the Month' award – a prestigious award for the catering community. One day as the 'Cook of the Month' himself was ladling out the food, one of B Squadron's old hands, Charlie C, leaned forward to liberate a chip from the serving tray. 'Cook of the Month' took exception to this and smartly whacked the back of Charlie's hand with the ladle. Charlie, who is not someone to upset if one can possibly help it, immediately grasped the hand of the cook and pressed it briefly but firmly onto the hotplate!

On another occasion we had come back at dawn from a long OP and we all trooped into the cookhouse to make ourselves a 'brew' and possibly an egg banjo or two. Tak was exceptionally hungry, so he opened the freezer, took out a whole frozen chicken, placed it in a chip basket and plunged it into the chip fryer. This was Fijian fast food at its finest!

We were very fortunate in B Squadron to have five Fijians – all of them legends. Tak seemed to attract trouble – but successfully. He had acted with great aggression and gallantry at Mirbat, receiving a big hole in his back and earning himself a Distinguished Conduct Medal (DCM) in the process. Well over a decade later, after he had left the British Army, he was working as a member of a security patrol for a private military company (PMC) in Iraq. One day some insurgents in a passing vehicle fired at Tak's vehicle and then pulled in front to force him to stop. This was a very foolish thing to do. Tak's vehicle screeched to a stop beside the other vehicle, he jumped out and promptly shot two of the insurgents and proceeded to beat the remaining attacker with the butt of his MP5. This was despite receiving another bullet wound to add to his collection.

Tak's Fijian compatriots in B Squadron in the 1970s and early 1980s were Jim V with a Military Medal; Tom M with a George Medal; Fred M with a British Empire Medal (BEM); and Laba Laba with a posthumous Mentioned in Dispatches. After leaving the British Army, Fred carved himself an amazing reputation as a door gunner on one of Executive Outcome's Hind helicopters fighting the rebels in Sierra Leone including assisting on Operation *Barras* – this was a true case of the 'old' SAS lion assisting younger 'Pilgrims' and Paras. I am very proud to have known all of these warriors, except Laba Laba whom sadly I never met, and to call them my friends.

While in the SAS, and unusually for an officer, I also had the opportunity to attend a patrol medics course. I was attached to a major hospital in the Midlands which was a fascinating experience. The SAS medical training I had undergone at Hereford beforehand was extremely comprehensive and the hospital staff had every confidence in my ability. Here I was able to carry out minor medical procedures that were usually the remit of doctors.

I normally started my day in Accident and Emergency and then the Infirmary would organise for me to visit various elements of the hospital. It was a teaching hospital and so all the medical staff were extremely welcoming and helpful. This attachment had been going on for several years and the hospital staff always welcomed the presence of SAS personnel. I have always been interested in the medical side of life so I entered into this course with great enthusiasm and I also knew that I had a forthcoming tour to Belize. There I would be fully responsible for the health and operational ability of the SAS group on its tour. This was a polyglot team, of troop size, from B Squadron – called, in-country, F Troop. However, my enthusiasm did have a downside. I would be rung up at all hours if there was a major emergency or if an 'interesting' situation had arisen at the hospital. I was certainly not complaining but I did feel a bit like a ghoul, not to mention knackered at the end of each day. I helped deliver babies, assisted with suturing patients in surgery, fixed broken limbs and sat with sick patients. It is certainly a tough profession to be in – my life then, and still to this day, is involved with fit healthy men but a hospital has every type of unwell humanity.

Once when I was on duty in Accident and Emergency, I was suturing a lady with a scalp wound and I had injected a quantity of Novocain into the scalp area. The Novocain pooled and so when I inserted the suturing needle I was covered in bloody gore spurting from her scalp. She was unaware of this and so was I. After I had completed the suturing, I thanked her, and opened the curtain of the little booth we were in, so she could leave. The waiting patients sitting in the chairs in the surrounding area looked absolutely horrified. A nurse quickly appeared and suggested very diplomatically that I pop into the bathroom nearby. Looking into the bathroom mirror I discovered that my face and gown were covered in blood. I must have looked like one of Count Dracula's henchmen as I came out of that booth.

TOUR TO BELIZE, 1979

In 1979 I went to Belize to command the SAS F Troop which was based there with the roulement British Battalion at Airport Camp. Belize, which was known as British Honduras until 1971, had on-going border tensions with Guatemala for some years and so there was a continual British Army and RAF presence. The RAF had some Harrier jets there and several Puma helicopters. Our task was to establish OPs on possible Guatemalan Special Forces infiltration routes. The Guatemalan Special Forces had been trained by the US Army. We also checked on caches that had been inserted by previous SAS patrols to ensure that they were still in good condition. These caches were to be used by SAS stay-behind patrols in the event of hostilities breaking out. We were never convinced about the utility of these caches because they were normally about ten days' travel apart – bear in mind how difficult the Belize jungle is to move through – but only contained rations and equipment for five days. Work that one out! The caches were often unserviceable due to water ingress, pigs having dug them up, or sometimes locals having already found them. The locals, and the pigs, must have thought they had found manna from heaven. We also had the odd OP task on the roads in the rural areas where it was believed that small aircraft were landing to deliver drugs into the country. We never came across any aircraft landing, so we were never sure of the reliability of this 'intelligence'.

Occasionally, we would spend a few days' leave on one of the idyllic islands just off the coast of Belize. Our favourite was Caye Caulker which in those days was completely unspoiled and not well known. We would travel to the island on a wooden pirogue with an enormous outboard engine captained by 'Chocolate', a permanently smiling local boatman.

We would take our rations and sleep on hammocks beside the beach. The locals were very friendly, particularly when Fred M would take off his sweat rag, hook it around a coconut tree and shin straight up it to collect coconuts for them and us. This was obviously an old Fijian trick but even more impressive was Fred's ability to husk a coconut in a few seconds flat! The locals were very impressed. They were less impressed when they suspected us of releasing the turtles they had lined up, upside down, on the beach with string through holes punched through their fore-flippers. We would see these turtles swimming in the ocean as we swam over the nearby reefs. Friendly, harmless creatures, but to a Belizean, they were dinner. Fred also introduced us to his specialty, 'melon surprise'. This was a melon in which a hole had been cut and into the hole was poured the contents of at least one bottle of 'Barrel' rum. Belize had numerous brands of rum but the affordable 'Barrel' rum came in three types – 'One Barrel', 'Two Barrel' and 'Three Barrel'. If I recall, 'One Barrel' was the cheapest and most potent. At some stage, decided by Fred, the melon would be opened, and the contents drunk/eaten. This drink made Fred smile even more than his usual broad grin. I enjoyed Fred's melon surprises – I think!

The terrain in Belize is very difficult with endless limestone mountains with no connecting ridgelines. We called it 'egg-box' country. Any cut or abrasion was guaranteed to become infected in 24 hours. One of the more unpleasant diseases was leishmaniasis which is caused by the bite of certain types of sandflies and leaves gaping ulcerous holes in the faces and bodies of its victims. Gurkha troops serving in Belize were particularly susceptible to this infection and it is difficult to treat.

Following a jungle patrol one of the troop, nicknamed 'The Toad', had noticed a small worm appearing out of the inside of his thigh. It was diagnosed as a 'pear worm' parasite. The eggs of this worm are laid by flies on a human host. The egg hatches while still living in the host until the host's skin eventually erupts into a massive boil and the worm crawls out. Its lower body is the size of the tip of a little finger and is much bigger than its head. If you try to pull the worm out it will break, and the remaining parts will cause a massive infection. 'The Toad' was duly taken into the small operating theatre in Airport Camp and the duty military doctor, surrounded by Toad's interested SAS colleagues, proceeded to cut this particular worm out. It was very hot and stuffy in the operating room and we all started to feel a little queasy as the doctor dug into Toad's thigh. Toad was being extraordinarily staunch throughout the proceedings. The worm was successfully removed and placed in a metal dish and the doctor proceeded to suture the quite large wound. Suddenly there was a great shriek which immediately terminated our queasiness and Toad almost leapt off the operating bench. It seemed that the doctor had mistaken one of Toad's pubic hairs for the black suturing thread and given it an almighty pull.

One of our tasks in Belize was to patrol the Sarstoon River which marked the southern border with Guatemala. We had three very imposing black Gemini inflatable boats with large 40-horsepower Johnson motors on the back. We also had one 9-horsepower 'spare' engine. At the start of the patrol we negotiated the tricky breakers at the entrance to the Sarstoon River and roared past the crew of the Guatemalan gunboat permanently moored on their side of the river. We made sure that we all looked suitably well armed and warlike. Unfortunately, some seven days later we sheepishly putted past the same gunboat with the lead Gemini powered only by the 9-horsepower motor towing the other two inflatables with their inoperative 40-horsepower Johnsons sitting silently on their sterns. This was after two replacement Johnsons had already been brought to us by helicopter when we were further up the river. We did not dare look at the Guatemalan sailors – it was too embarrassing.

There must have been some strong Ministry of Defence loyalty to Johnsons because some years later at the beginning of the Falklands War during the initial abortive South Georgia raid an SAS boat troop operation ended up with their Johnsons failing. The crews were drifting silently and freezingly towards the Antarctic before they were rescued.

Fred, who was also my troop sergeant, and I decided to take a bus from Belize City to the border with Mexico and spend a few days' leave visiting Chetumal, an ancient Mayan capital and port at the entrance to the Hondo River, the border with Belize. We obtained the appropriate visas from the Mexican Embassy and we set off on the bus from the brilliantly named Batty Bus Company which made a regular run to the Mexican border. The Belizeans had an expression 'No big 'ting mun, no big 'ting' and this was how any delay or problem was managed. The bus, loaded with people, chickens, crates, baskets and you name it, took many hours to reach Mexico.

Each of the windows of the bus was held up by pieces of wood but every so often one of these bits of wood would fall out and the window would slam shut with a noise like a gunshot. All the passengers, most of whom had been dozing, would scream and jump into the air in fright. This, combined with the casual air of nonchalance affected by the driver as he hammered the bus around blind corners on the wrong side of the road, made it a somewhat traumatic journey.

We finally left the bus at the Belize border and walked across the steel bridge over the Hondo River to the Mexican border post. There two Mexican immigration and customs officials waited, complete with Zapata moustaches, tight trousers and their high Texan-style cowboy boots resting on the counter. Hung low on their hips were gunbelts encasing rows of bullets and each holding a large silver six-gun. We greeted them in our best Spanish and received a non-committal 'Si' in response. I showed them my passport and visa and was given the OK to proceed. But with Fred there was a problem. He was the proud holder of a Fijian passport complete with a visa for Mexico which we had obtained from their embassy in Belize City. Fiji had gained independence from Britain in 1970, but, unfortunately, our border officials could not find Fiji in their 'book of countries' which had obviously not been updated for many years. Fred was therefore simply not permitted into Mexico. So, we trudged back across the bridge to Belize. We then spent the next 24 hours going back and forth across this damned bridge to try to convince the officials to let us into Mexico. In the end, a sympathetic customs officer took us on a half-day tour to see the sights and grand Mexican monuments of Chetumal in his own car before returning us back to the border post and our favourite bridge.

At the completion of this Belize tour I returned to Hereford, finished my SAS posting and was then posted, on promotion to major, to command A Company 1 Para based in Aldershot. An officer in the SAS would normally do three years initially as a troop commander. The officer then returned to his parent unit. If selected he could return later as a major and command a squadron.

I was very privileged to have spent nearly four years with 22 SAS commanding 8 Troop, the mobility troop of B Squadron. I believed then, and still do to this day, that the mainstay of the SAS remains its troopers, junior NCOs and young officers. They are what makes the SAS so successful.

I had received excellent annual confidential reports throughout my tour with 22 SAS, and I was informed by a senior officer, just before I finally left to go to Aldershot, that I was 'shortlisted' as one of the future commanding officers of 22 SAS. However, this was not to be.

5

1ST BATTALION, THE PARACHUTE REGIMENT, 1980-81

I joined 1 Para late in 1979 and the battalion was based at Bruneval Barracks in Aldershot where I had been with 3 Para. When I was in 3 Para the commanding officer had not been very popular and some large graffiti had been painted on one of the main walls of the 'covered way' – this was a part of the barracks where we could load vehicles and equipment etc. under cover. It was hastily painted over at the time by the 3 Para provost staff. I was amused to see now some four years later that the graffiti was again emerging through its camouflaging paint. The CO was a thin aesthetic man, but was and still is an extraordinary long-distance runner. When I first joined 3 Para Patrol Company, I was told with great glee how, before my time, when the CO had been the officer commanding Patrol Company on an exercise in Cyprus he had overlooked his Sterling sub-machine gun and the Toms buried it! I do not believe that it was ever found but he must have managed to get away with its loss. This may be an apocryphal story, but it was certainly retold to me with great sincerity. This particular CO was not fond of the SAS and was not pleased when I left 3 Para to join them.

It was very interesting joining 1 Para and being back in the 'normal' regimental system. The previous OC of A Company had been an American exchange officer and he had fitted in well although soon after joining the company he badly broke his leg in a parachuting accident and spent a great deal of his time in a plaster cast. My company sergeant major (CSM) was Paul C, a very serious but professional SNCO who later received a Q Commission. He was replaced by 'Flash' F, another really professional SNCO with a good sense of humour who was also later commissioned. My NCOs were a good team and we soon formed a very tight-knit group. My NCOs and soldiers were, as Field Marshal Montgomery described, 'every man an emperor' – Ivor Pringle, Andy Warner, Kev Whittle, Ray Toon, Barry Waters, Sean Johnson, Gaz Grant, Stu Aitkin, Andy Gough – but I always had to keep my wits about me with them! I knew I had a bit of work to do when I was checking the platoons prior to departing on our first field training exercise together and saw one of the Toms with a tray of fresh eggs balanced on his bergen. How he expected to be able to patrol in full webbing and carrying a heavy bergen and his rifle, as well as these eggs, I do not know. As always, the Toms were great; they worked really hard, disliked inactivity and could take anything that was thrown at them but with the inevitable downside – they played hard! One of the things I implemented was the wearing of camouflage, disruptive pattern material (DPM) trousers with the Para smock and a camouflage cap with hessian attached. This did lead to some of the other companies calling A Company 'Bob Marley's wailers' because the hessian on our caps looked like Rastafarian curls. I am a great believer in personal camouflage, it is a lifesaver. If the enemy has difficulty seeing you, he is likely to have difficulty in shooting you. Interestingly, I was criticised by the CO because he said, I quote, 'Paras should always wear denims (green trousers), smock and beret for identification'. This was unsurprising; my new CO, despite being an airborne officer, lacked initiative or flair. I was glad not to have to go to war with him.

I had two lieutenant platoon commanders and rode them hard. I wasn't particularly liked by them as a result but they both went on to have excellent army careers. One, John Y, was later badly injured in the Falklands War, but then, through sheer determination recovered to pass 22 SAS selection, becoming first a troop and then a squadron commander. The other, Simon S, commanded troops in Oman and then became an extremely successful businessman working in some of the most dangerous parts of the world.

HONG KONG, 1980

In 1980, 1 Para was posted to Hong Kong for several months to man the border area with the People's Republic of China. This was a job normally done by the Gurkhas, but they were to be withdrawn for their annual training. The border area, which was closed to civilian access, ran beside an area of no man's land between Hong Kong and China. Very large numbers of illegal immigrants (IIs), known as 'eye-eyes', would attempt to cross the gap between the two countries.

At that time, the Hong Kong government allowed illegal immigrants to obtain residency if they were able to present themselves at certain locations in the centre of Hong Kong or Kowloon. This was known as a 'home run'. This policy was designed to stop a subculture of illegal immigrants within Hong Kong. This did, however, present an incentive to the 'runners'. Along the high ground overlooking the border were large bunkers with battlements called MacKenzie forts (I liked that name!) and in these lived a section of soldiers whose job was to patrol the high ground and intercept the illegal immigrants coming into Hong Kong. The border area had a high, razor wire-topped fence running the length of the border with a road running parallel with it. Unfortunately, the road was on the outside of the fence. This fence had a number of locked gates allowing access through it, but if any illegal immigrant was seen climbing a fence the military patrol had to run to the nearest gate, unlock it and then locate the 'runners' who were, by now, over a mile away. The 'runners' were well briefed and, at night, would climb a part of the fence as far away from the access gates as possible. Despite the razor wire, the illegal immigrants could cross the fence in minutes. They would wear excess clothing to protect themselves from the wire and slip off the clothing as it got caught in the barbs, rather like a snake shedding its skin.

My company was based at the police station in Sha Tau Kok. This was a small fishing village, which was bisected by the eastern end of the border between Hong Kong and China. The actual border was a line in the paving in the middle of the street. A glowering PRC (People's Republic of China) soldier, complete with AKM rifle, stood on one side of the street and we stood on the other. Beside the police station was a dug-in platoon defensive position on the high ground dominating the village and the border crossing point. On 8 July 1967, during rioting in Hong Kong instigated by the Chinese Cultural Revolution, hundreds of armed militia from the People's Republic of China had fired at the Hong Kong police at Sha Tau Kok. Five policemen were killed in the brief exchange of fire. After this attack both the police station and the defensive position were built.

My company headquarters was based in the police station with one of my platoons, another platoon was based in the defended location nearby and the third platoon was spread along the hills in the MacKenzie forts. The platoon in the defensive position essentially had to live underground. One of my NCOs, 'Big' Danny Keown, was the original troglodyte and thrived in this underground complex.

We took over from a Gurkha company and before they left we carried out a number of combined patrols with them. Along the border fence itself we had to work a reverse daily routine, patrolling by night and resting by day. Patrols would go to night locations at known or likely crossing points and await the movement of the illegals as they attempted during the night to cross from China into Hong Kong. Most of the Paras had not worked with Gurkhas before, gauging them on their impressive World War II reputation. Sadly, the Gurkhas we worked with were lazy and slovenly. Once they had consumed their nightly issue tot of rum they got into their sleeping bags and went to sleep. Their OP areas were filthy with rubbish and human waste. On one of these combined patrols a Gurkha was in the process of arresting an 'eye-eye' but got himself into a panic and managed to spray himself directly in the face with a can of mace. We had to organise his medical evacuation. My Paras were appalled, and their previous image of the Gurkhas was shattered. The Gurkha officers were an anachronism and were lorded over by their batmen and waiters. We were not sorry to see them, and their men, leave.

Each day, at dusk, on the hills along the Chinese side of the border little groups of eye-eyes could be seen gathering like Comanche Indians on the tops of the hills. As it became dark, they would filter down towards the Chinese border troops on their side of the border. We would hear shouts, screams and dogs barking; see lights flashing and hear an occasional shot being fired. Then there would be silence. But in the early hours of the morning rustling would be heard in the overgrown area between the two borders as groups and individuals would start creeping towards the Hong Kong side. My patrols would wait in ambush and apprehend these eye-eyes as they tried to cross the road and scale the fence. There were more eye-eyes than we had patrols so quite a few eluded us. The eye-eyes were never violent and would wait patiently to be taken back to the police station. Next day they would be collected by the Hong Kong police transport and at some stage they would be repatriated back to China through the border crossing point at Lo Wu. During our tour we apprehended several whom we had already caught before.

I enjoyed this period because the company was very much left alone and the visits from battalion headquarters based in Fan Ling were few and far between. However, because of Sha Tau Kok's strategic location, we did receive several high-powered political visitors from the United Kingdom who wanted to see first-hand how the 'eye-eye' prevention programme was working.

The country on the Hong Kong side behind the border fence was steep and hilly so I introduced daylight mounted horse patrols so that we could cover more ground. The first problem was teaching a number of the company to ride. We were fortunate in that relatively close to the border was a riding school which had many fine horses, the majority of which were former racehorses.

We spent quite a bit of time riding around and around the training ring under the very strict supervision of a fearsome lady instructor. She took no nonsense from the Toms – or anyone else. She would have made an excellent regimental sergeant major. We were taught how to saddle the horses and learned all about the the tricks the horses used to make it as difficult as possible to put them in harness. They could be very cunning and mischievous beasts. Then the great day came, and we set off on our first outing. My horse was called 'Thunder' – that should have given me some warning about his nature. His party trick was suddenly to stop and lower his head; his rider, unless fully alert, would slide quickly and dramatically over Thunder's head onto the ground. If the reins were not tightly gripped Thunder would then trot happily back to the stables.

The initial patrols were very successful but one of the main difficulties was training the Toms not to steer the horses like a motorbike and to accept that horses were very intelligent and could avoid obstacles themselves.

As former racehorses, these particular mounts remained fiercely competitive. This was not a problem when we set off on our day-long patrols, but it certainly was on our return. The return journey was mainly downhill along small paths and the horses knew exactly when we had turned for home. They would get a glint in their eyes and start moving faster and faster until they were almost galloping. This was despite the ineffectual input from the Para on board. As we got closer to the stables the paths had sharper and sharper corners and the horses were now racing their companions. At nearly every corner there would be an aggrieved Para painfully getting up off the ground having been flung off. The final turn was from the dirt path onto the tar-sealed road leading into the stables. Here the horses slid and careered amidst sparks and stones as they took this final corner home. I think only about 50 per cent of each patrol managed to return home still on their original horse. I now know horses can look smug because I have seen them!

We were on the border during Easter so 'Flash', my CSM, and I sat up all day painting boiled eggs so that we could give one to every soldier in the company. I am not sure they appreciated it but at least they knew that we in the 'head-shed' were thinking of them. Delivering the eggs to the MacKenzie forts, like any visit to them, proved to be a little hazardous. The forts were on the top of very sharply inclined ridge lines and steep steps had to be climbed to reach them. Every so often a raw potato would come hurtling down through the air. This was obviously one of the sporting activities – try to hit the OC and/or the CSM with a potato volley. Needless to say, whoever was in charge of the post denied all knowledge of any potato missiles.

The leave policy we had in Hong Kong for the troops was badly thought out and not particularly generous. The Toms were only allowed two-and-a-half days' leave every three weeks or so. They would go on leave into Kowloon or Hong Kong Island from a rest camp away from the border area. The Toms had been working hard and inevitably they played hard but added to this equation was the fact that the resident battalion was the Queen's Own Highlanders based in Stanley Fort on Hong Kong Island and commanded by my namesake Lieutenant Colonel Jeremy MacKenzie. The Paras and the Jocks took to each other with a passion and kept the Hong Kong police busy with their antics. It even reached the stage where the rest of the army wore T-shirts in town stating, 'I am NOT from 1 PARA' so they would be allowed into the bars and nightclubs. I could never understand why the CO found all this surprising. I did not condone the excesses of some individuals but if you train Paras to be extremely aggressive for a potential war role then you mustn't be too surprised if they do not behave like saints in peacetime. The core attributes and aggression of Paras would be demonstrated most ably not long afterwards in the Falklands War.

The CO had also decreed that no soldiers were to have tattoos in Hong Kong because of the high incidence of Hepatitis B. In their own inimitable way, the Toms took this as rather a personal challenge. The first I knew of any 'disobedience' of this order was when we were having a farewell BBQ kindly arranged by the local police inspector at his house just on the outskirts of the border area. The Toms had had a few beers and were becoming somewhat boisterous, so it was a good time for the BBQ to finish and for us to return to our duties. Almost as one, about 20 of the Toms formed a line, turned away and mooned the assembled officers and senior NCOs. On each of their right backsides was a tattoo of a pink 'Lil' Devil' holding a pitchfork and wearing Para wings. The CSM and I decided to ignore this little display of independence and the subject of tattoos was never mentioned in A Company again.

RETURN TO THE UNITED KINGDOM

Following the tour in Hong Kong, the company returned with the battalion to Aldershot and we continued on with company training. I took the company to Salisbury Plains and we worked in Imber Village, which had originally been requisitioned during World War II as a training area and had now been converted into an urban training area. We practised using Molotov cocktails and other devices against buildings and vehicles. We also took the opportunity to test the 66mm anti-tank rocket as an anti-sniper weapon in a built-up area. It wasn't very successful, but it showed how the rocket worked in an area which was quite different from the normal sterile anti-tank range. All these activities, while realistic, would have given the range staff the 'vapours' if they had known about them.

We were required to carry out a certain number of parachute descents each year to remain 'current' but it was somewhat difficult to obtain RAF aircraft, so we used a balloon to jump onto Queens Avenue beside our camp. This was a good PR exercise as many civilians drove past the area. But none of us enjoyed jumping from the balloon; it was always eerily quiet except for the wind moaning through the balloon's wire hawsers. In an aircraft there is a lot more going on to distract you. Besides, when you jump out of an aircraft you are swept along by a 120-knot slipstream rather than simply dropping like a brick as you do out of a balloon.

We jumped with our equipment containers from the balloon and this was an interesting experience because once you left the balloon cage you plummeted straight down incredibly fast thanks to the extra weight. More than once, if I had been able to find my reserve handle I would have pulled it because looking up my parachute seemed to take forever to deploy, but it was simply the long dropping sensation. On some occasions my family, who were living in military quarters nearby, would come and watch this balloon parachuting. I would look over the side of the balloon basket and see them as little dots 800 feet below. It felt good that I could share a little of my 'airborne' experiences with them.

On our defensive training exercises I tried to convince the company of the benefits of the DuPuy trench system. This is a defensive trench system where each defensive position defends the adjoining position by firing across its front. This was used very successfully by the Wehrmacht in Italy and elsewhere during World War II. Attacking troops were hit by enfilade fire as they assaulted each position. I had to compromise, however, and allow limited vision to the front of each trench. The Toms were simply not happy at not being able to see to their own front.

My final exercise with the battalion was at Camp Wainwright in Canada. This is a vast live-firing infantry training area infested by the biggest, angriest midges in the world! They could teach the feared Scottish midges a thing or two. One of the facilities at Wainwright was an underground defence position which the company occupied for several days. The Toms did not like living underground like moles and it was a full-time job for the senior NCOs to stop them sticking their heads out of their bunkers like Meerkats whenever they could. During the time in Canada I was assisted by a former SAS SNCO, Mick H, who was to be commissioned into the SAS permanent cadre. He contributed a great deal to the company's training and at the end of the training he and I took the opportunity to tour the Rockies in a hire car.

It was on this exercise in Canada that I finally became disillusioned by the way the army training was going and especially the lack of imagination on the part of the battalion's commanding officer. There was absolutely no drive or vision in the grooming of our soldiers for war. Peacetime soldiering, discounting the futility of operations in Northern Ireland, had taken its toll on the Parachute Regiment.

I decided to seek soldiering opportunities elsewhere. This was despite receiving an almost unheard of direct entry to the Army Command and Staff College at Camberley. This had been given to only one previous officer and that was General Sir Peter de la Billière KCB, KBE, DSO, MC and Bar. This was a huge compliment to me and had taken a great deal of lobbying by various officers in the SAS and the Parachute Regiment. I regret letting those people down to this day, but the thought of continuing to soldier in such a sterile and depressing environment was not for me. I had been in touch with the South African Defence Attaché in London, and after much correspondence, I was offered an appointment in the parachute brigade of the South African Defence Force (SADF).

However, before my official departure there was a formal duty I had to perform. I had the honour and the privilege of commanding a Parachute Regiment hundred-man Royal Guard of Honour for her Majesty the Queen Mother on 6 June 1980. The Queen Mother was unveiling a bronze statue of Field Marshal Bernard Montgomery on the Mall. We rehearsed in London under the watchful eye of the Grenadier Guards RSM who was obviously miffed that this Royal Guard was not being provided from the Foot Guards.

The great moment came, and the guard was drawn up and honours presented. The Queen Mother, escorted by Field Marshal Edwin Brammall, Baron Brammall, stepped from the dais to walk over and unveil the statue. Field Marshal Brammall, a short individual, tripped over his sword and pitched onto the ground. My heart sank – this was just the sort of thing that would have Paras in paroxysms of laughter. It just needed one person to start laughing, and the Guard of Honour would have dissolved into chaos – just like the scene with the centurions in the film *The Life of Brian*.

I wondered whether I would have to cleave with my sword the first one to crack. To my eternal gratitude there was not a sound from the ranks behind me. The field marshal dusted himself off and the event continued without further drama. The South African defence attaché, who was one of the VIP guests, later complimented me on the high standard of the parade as did the Grenadier Guards RSM, albeit somewhat ungraciously.

6

44 SOUTH AFRICAN PARACHUTE BRIGADE (THE PARABATS), 1981-82

In January 1981 I resigned from the British Army, handed over my military quarters in Aldershot and set off for the Republic of South Africa. My family had returned to New Zealand while I set up in South Africa.

I was originally recruited to assist the South African Special Forces in the development of their counterterrorism capability. I was, therefore, somewhat surprised to receive a posting order to 1 Para in Tempe, the depot of the South African Defence Force (SADF) parachute forces, in Bloemfontein. This posting was then changed to the headquarters of 44 Parachute Brigade which is where I finally arrived. Some months after being in the SADF I had an interview with General F.W. Loots, the commander of South African Special Forces. At our meeting I queried why I was not posted to the Special Forces as had been originally planned. I reminded him that I had top-secret security clearance in the SADF. He paused and said, 'Ah – but there is many a slip between the cup and the lip.' He made it quite clear that he thought I was a British spy.

Most of the permanent force in the SADF spoke Afrikaans as their first language, although they were all bilingual in English too. At this time all official documents had to be in both Afrikaans and English. This included military pamphlets and handbooks. Military correspondence, however, alternated monthly between Afrikaans and English. Inevitably, what happened was that Afrikaans speakers, in the English month, dated everything as of the last day of the Afrikaans month, and vice versa. So, everyone simply continued to write correspondence in their own primary language.

I learned basic Afrikaans before travelling to South Africa but luckily my limitations in the language were not a problem in the brigade headquarters as English was the main language used.

Soon after arriving at my brigade headquarters I met my new commanding officer, the legendary Colonel Jan Breytenbach. He welcomed me warmly and showed me around the 'farm' at Murrayhill, Hammanskraal, some 30 miles north of Pretoria. The farm, which was literally just that, was a minimalist environment, but the farm, outhouses and store rooms were filled with stores, ammunition and soft-skin vehicles.

There was some accommodation in a small building and this was occupied by the 44 Parachute Brigade Headquarters Pathfinder Company. This unique little band of men was composed mainly of foreign nationals most of whom had served in the Rhodesian forces prior to joining the SADF. Alongside the Rhodesians, there were Americans, including several Vietnam veterans, Brits, Australians and a Kiwi and later, if I recall correctly, the company was also joined by Frenchmen and a Spaniard. I was the new officer commanding the Pathfinders Company, as well as the brigade's second-in-command and almost everything else in between.

It was a colourful mob, to be sure, and made no less so by the mutual animosity between two sergeant majors of the unit. One was Pete McAleese, and the other was Frank Green. McAleese had come from the British SAS as well as the Rhodesian SAS, and was, naturally, a formidable character. Green was a one-legged Rhodesian, a former racing driver, whose speciality was designing Q vehicles. These were civilian vehicles, but concealed machine guns and other weapons. McAleese and Green did not get on. At one stage, in the middle of the bush when the unit was travelling overland from Pretoria to deploy to South West Africa, Green and McAleese had a stand-up brawl in front of the rather bemused troops.

A British couple, Clive and Alyson Lea-Cox, who had joined the SADF before me kindly offered to let me board with them until I could find suitable accommodation and so I was able to move out of the hotel in Pretoria that I had been staying in – there was no military accommodation. Clive had been the CO of a county regiment and Alyson had been a Women's Royal Army Corps (WRAC) officer and they had met while serving in Northern Ireland. After several months, my family was able to join me but trying to get accommodation continued to be a problem. The SADF, like some other armies, allocated points based on an officer's length of service and these points go towards housing allocation. But, in my case, because my previous service was not in the SADF I was not allocated any points and so would never be eligible for military housing. At one stage for a short while we lived in a small *rondavel* (thatched hut) on the Para Brigade farm at Hammanskraal with no electricity and minimal facilities. My two children remember it mostly because of the enormous spiders which also occupied the rondavel and came out at night to forage by the light of the candles.

I was eventually able to rent a small duplex apartment on the outskirts of Pretoria and it was a relief to have a firm base for the family. I could now concentrate on the job in hand.

———

Firstly, I needed to familiarise myself with South African kit and equipment. Soon after I arrived Colonel Breytenbach took me to visit the DSIR (Department for Scientific and Industrial Research) workshops in Pretoria which were assisting in the development of the Pathfinder specialist vehicles – the Jackals. He introduced me to the imposing SADF Ratel (honey badger) armoured vehicle. He showed me around the vehicle and finally, with a mischievous smile, pointed to a large rusty grille that was bolted to the rear left-hand side of the vehicle, and said, 'What do you think that is?' When I looked completely puzzled he laughed loudly and said, 'That's the *braai*! [BBQ] You could only get that in the SADF!'

The Armaments Corporation of South Africa, or Armscor, worked closely with the Department for Scientific and Industrial Research. Essentially the military would define a requirement and Armscor would examine it and farm the project out to the company or companies with the necessary expertise, giving assistance as required. A prototype would be developed and handed to military personnel who tested it and reported their findings. Modifications were made as necessary and if a further test did not indicate more modifications Armscor allocated the manufacture. The development of SADF equipment was probably the most rapid in the world – a piece of equipment could be tested and conclusions given in a matter of days rather than months and years as in most other countries.

The Pathfinder Company's main requirement at this time was for a light, air-portable, air-droppable, cross-country vehicle which could carry sufficient logistic support for a four-man crew and have fire support powerful enough to allow vehicles to operate behind enemy lines in Angola, and on internal operations in South West Africa, as South Africa's Border War was now at its height. The terrain that the Pathfinders would be operating in was very sandy and flat with areas of riverbeds or *shonas* cutting through the area. These shonas fill with about 18 inches of water in the wet season. Throughout the area were clumps of the distinctive flat-topped mopane trees with their savage thorns, home to tiny black flies that feast on the liquid in one's eyes and mouth. The mopane copses were surrounded by barriers of thick thorny scrub. Where the mopane trees were cut down there was left a razor-sharp stump, which could rip the tyre off a vehicle.

The DSIR had taken the lead in designing the esoteric vehicles needed for South Africa's Border War, known more colloquially as the Bush War. The Buffel (*buffel* meaning buffalo), armoured personnel carrier, which was a masterpiece of the art of mine-proofing vehicles, and the Ratel infantry combat vehicle were both designed in the workshops of the DSIR. Frank Green had previously been involved in the design and operation of Q vehicles in Rhodesia with Special Forces Headquarters. Although he had lost a leg in a motor racing accident, Frank was a great machine gunner on the battlefield and became a dynamic and enthusiastic member of the design team for the Jackal.

The Jackal was based upon the British ¾-ton Land Rover and also on Toyota Land Cruisers. Eight vehicles were received; they were stripped down and the mechanics thoroughly checked. All the panel work was removed and the chassis strengthened by welding and bolting alloy bars under the seats in the front. Duplicate fuel tanks were placed behind the existing tanks and all tanks were filled with multi-mesh aluminium to stop the fuel exploding in the event of a strike by an incendiary round. The next step was the placing of a mesh grille over the engine compartment to protect it; after initial trials, this grille had to have a canvas screen placed underneath to stop grass seed from the *veldt* (open, rural landscape of southern Africa) clogging the engine air intakes. A solid tray of ¾-inch steel was fixed over the rear axle; this was to be the gun platform. Various trays could be fitted on to the platform dependent upon the weapon required, including 106mm recoilless rifles; a .50-calibre machine gun or twin 7.62 MAGS – the Belgium machine gun.

There were no doors or windscreens, but a grille was provided to protect the driver and the commander in the front from the savage thorny vegetation found in the operational area. Boxes for radios were situated between the driver and the commander. There were three radios per vehicle: one radio for inter-vehicle communications; one to speak to foot patrols; and the frequency-hopping set for the link to the tactical headquarters. Storage bins were placed to the rear of the driver and commander. On the rear and sides, jerry cans with fuel were clamped on the racks. These cans were connected to a quick release device. If the cans were ignited, the number two gunner pulled and pushed the lever and the cans fell away. There was another extra that was unique. This was the smoke dispenser based on the Soviet method for producing smoke from armoured vehicles. A small container of brake fluid was placed over the exhaust manifold and this container had a valve connected to a tap on the dashboard. When the tap was opened, the fluid would drip onto the manifold and clouds of dense white smoke would issue from the exhaust pipe. The system gave each vehicle the ability to lay down a screen for the quick and effective protection of itself or to cover the manoeuvre of others.

The weapons affixed to the vehicles depended upon the role that vehicle would be required to carry out on operations and the type of enemy likely to be encountered. To engage enemy infantry, the Belgian 7.62 mm MAG was the tried and tested favourite. A twin MAG was mounted on a pedestal behind a metal shrapnel shield. Each MAG had a 500-round box welded to the side of the pedestal and empty cases, or *doppies*, were collected in a sack beneath each gun. This was to stop them rolling around on the floor causing gunners to lose their footing. Other vehicles were armed with a .50-calibre Browning for anti-vehicle work using mixed belts of armour-piercing, armour-piercing incendiary, and ball ammunition. One vehicle even had twin .50-calibre Brownings mounted but accuracy suffered as the platform did not remain stable when the weapons were fired. Another experiment involved mounting a 20mm cannon 'liberated' from a South African Air Force (SAAF) Canberra bomber. The cannon had excellent range and penetration but there were problems with the cooling and recoil system as it was, obviously, designed for use on an aircraft.

The vehicles were required to carry a team of four as the Pathfinders were organised into patrols of four men as in the British SAS: a driver responsible for the mobility of the vehicle; a commander who had a pintle-mounted MAG in front of him, responsible for navigation and tactical deployment; a number one gunner responsible for the primary weapon; and a number two gunner whose task was to protect the gunner and take over in the event that the number one gunner became a casualty.

Vast amounts of stores had to be carried as patrols could be operating a long way from base. Apart from the rations and water for 14 days there were the business items. The SADF personal equipment was very good. The personal weapon was the 5.56mm R4 based on the Israeli Galil. The Para helmet was a direct copy of the Israeli version with a nutria-brown helmet cover with a peak – I had never worn a helmet with a peak before! Webbing was chest-mounted with some six magazine pouches. Personal weapons for the crew included the 5.56mm R4 and the Spanish 9mm Star automatic handguns (called the bush hammer because that was all they were good for!); M79 grenade launchers; RPG-7s; STRIM rocket launchers similar to the US 3.5 rocket launcher; and, of course, large amounts of ammunition. Specialist items included explosive and mines. It was particularly satisfying laying captured Soviet mines – this appealed to our rather strange sense of humour.

Also carried were flares, extra radio batteries and two spare vehicle tyres. All the tyres were filled with foam that kept the tyres inflated even when punctured by several rounds of AK-47 fire. Unfortunately, the foam was no match for the mopane stumps as we found out later. There was no mine protection on the vehicles because of weight restrictions and the only insurance against setting off a mine was sticking to operational procedures about avoiding tracks and roads, combined with the keen eyesight of the crew and the skill of the driver. This was not always successful!

After a four-month preparation, in early March 1981 the Jackals were ready to move to South West Africa. The move from the Pathfinder base in Pretoria to the operational area in South West Africa took seven days. This drive took the 'pack' of Jackals through the Republic of South Africa's then provinces of the Transvaal and the Orange Free State, and along the southern edge of Botswana and the Kalahari Desert. In the latter, the column was pounded by hailstones as big as golf balls. The column then proceeded through the eastern side of South West Africa to the SADF base at Grootfontein and then along the 'blacktop', the only sealed road in the north of South West Africa (Owamboland) to the final destination of Ondangwa, a large airbase in South West Africa, and the operational base for the Pathfinders. The base fell within Sector 10, one of three front-line 'sectors' of South West Africa directly controlled by the SADF. The Jackals had been thoroughly tested mechanically on this arduous journey and, except for a few minor problems, all were running well. One vehicle, however, had broken its back crossing a riverbed; this was welded together and, apart from a rather strange U-shaped profile, it was as good as new. Pathfinder operations were carried out from the Para Battalion base at Ondangwa which was a major airbase in South West Africa. The area military and civil administration was based in nearby Oshakati. The accommodation was very spartan and there were very few luxuries. We lived in large canvas tents with metal beds on the sand. The majority of manpower in South West Africa was provided by white national servicemen commanded by permanent force officers and senior NCOs. I noticed that the national servicemen were not treated particularly well by their permanent force counterparts.

My first task at 44 Brigade had been to formalise the selection and training of the Pathfinders. The training, up until that stage, had been organised by Sergeant Major Pete McAleese. It had been carried out enthusiastically and vigorously but needed some structure. I also undertook to write the formal Standard Operational Procedures (SOP) for the Pathfinder Company.

The current Pathfinders had a certain amount of combat experience, but their attitude to discipline, both on the field operations and in base, left a bit to be desired. This did not endear them to the more formal SADF. There was an animosity towards the Pathfinders in almost every area that we worked. We were very much regarded as Colonel Breytenbach's private army.

Colonel Breytenbach himself liked to lead from the front. He enjoyed going on operations with the soldiers in the Para Brigade and in particular with the Pathfinders in their Jackal vehicles into South West Africa and across the border into Angola. On one Pathfinder patrol he was very nearly killed when his Jackal vehicle ran over an anti-tank mine. The vehicle with its numerous fuel cans exploded in a ball of fire. He personally saved the machine gunner on the rear of the vehicle, Dave Barr, from the flames. All the occupants of the vehicle were injured, with Dave Barr losing both his legs, but no one was killed. You cannot get much closer to the action than that! I had found a commanding officer I would happily follow to war.

ON OPERATIONS WITH THE PATHFINDERS

The majority of Pathfinder operations I was involved in took place above the 'cut line' in Angola. The Bush War had first flared up due to the Namibian people's opposition to South Africa's mandate over South West Africa (modern-day Namibia). The opposition was provided by the People's Liberation Army of Namibia (PLAN), the armed wing of the South West Africa People's Organisation (SWAPO), although we generally referred to them simply as SWAPO rather than making the distinction. The conflict intensified when Angola, to the north of South West Africa, won its independence from Portugal in 1975. The left-wing Popular Movement for the Liberation of Angola (MPLA), with assistance from the Soviet Union and Cuba, came to power and immediately began offering support, in terms of physical bases inside Angola, to SWAPO. It was these bases that became a primary target for the SADF.

The border between Angola and South West Africa is first formed by the Kunene River which runs from its mouth in the Atlantic Ocean for just over 185 miles to the small border town of Ruacana. From there the border is formed by a dead-straight 'cut line', marked by a rusty fence and frequent large, triangular, numbered wooden trig points, which runs for 265 miles. It was in the area north of this that we would operate on 'external' operations, i.e. outside South West Africa and into Angolan territory.

We frequently worked on such operations with 32 'Buffalo' Battalion. This was a unit composed predominately of Portuguese-speaking black Angolans who had been recruited by Jan Breytenbach at the end of the Angolan War of Independence. As MPLA had secured power in the newly independent Angola, and was committed to a one-party state, some Angolans as well as other Angolan political parties looked for non-Soviet external assistance. The South African government would primarily support the

National Union for the Total Independence of Angola (UNITA). This meant that Angola rapidly developed into a vicious Cold War-era proxy war.

Some of the 32 Battalion NCOs and all the officers were permanent force members of the SADF. This unit was extremely aggressive and was probably one of the most effective units during the South African Bush War.

Like a lot of battle zones there was a great deal of wildlife. Not surprisingly there were few poachers and we would often come across elephant or herds of springbok or kudu and any waterholes were full of crocodiles (called 'flat dogs' by the South Africans) and hippos – two of the most dangerous creatures in Africa. A fellow Kiwi, Phil C, who with my assistance joined 32 Battalion, caused a great deal of concern to his colleagues when he returned to the 32 'Buffalo' Battalion camp at Rundu in the Caprivi Strip having been for a 'walkabout' and described how he had used their 'water slide' at the nearby river. His horrified companions explained to him that these slides were not made by playful soldiers frolicking in the river but by bloody great crocodiles and he was very, very lucky to still be intact!

The nights in the veldt are, as I was able to compare later in the deserts of Oman, absolutely stunning. The stars just go on forever and the silence is almost tangible. It was comforting at night to be able to look up and see the familiar Southern Cross star formation. This was helpful on more than one occasion when we were returning at night to South West Africa having carried out an operation above the 'cut line' in Angola – we just followed the 'Cross'.

As operations began with the Jackals, both inside and outside South West Africa, it quickly became apparent to us that the vehicles required a mother vehicle to provide reserve stores of fuel, food, water and, most importantly, ammunition. It was found that the Unimog 2.5 Mercedes was the most suitable truck available. Two of these vehicles were stripped right down, provided with a pintle-mounted MAG, extra fuel tanks and a pair of foam-filled spare tyres each. It was also decided to bolt a captured Soviet 14.5mm heavy machine gun on to the rear of another Unimog vehicle. Although designed as an anti-aircraft weapon, this machine gun was extremely efficient in the ground role with its fearsome rate of fire, and, of course, there was no shortage of captured ammunition.

The Jackals moved in pairs on operations with a twin MAG and a .50-calibre-equipped vehicle operating together. In some areas the scrub was too thick for the Jackals and one of the Unimog support vehicles would have to come forward and '*bundu*-bash' to make a passage for the much lower Jackal vehicles. (The Southern Africans called the 'bush' the *bundu* and to *bundu*-bash was to drive through the bush.) A typical operation, an external, would begin with the pack moving to a forward SADF base just south of the cut line. The attack headquarters would be set up and final briefings and rehearsals take place. Just before moving out, all weapons were test fired to ensure they functioned perfectly. Deployment would take place after last light avoiding waterholes, reservoirs and civilian *kraals*, or villages. If the move to the task area took more than one night the vehicles would be concealed during the day and the crews would rest, except for observation posts. If, however, the operation was to search and destroy then movement was by day so that *spoor* (enemy tracks) could be followed. If a fresh spoor was found, the enemy's likely destination was plotted while a pair of Jackals would move on a flank to cut off their route; the remainder of the pack would move parallel to the track and the enemy would be hunted down. We wore the brown SADF uniform in camp but in the field we dressed in camouflage clothing, either old Rhodesian camouflage or Portuguese camouflage clothing that we were issued from 32 Battalion.

The mission of one of our main raids into Angola in July 1981 was twofold: to destroy the main culvert bridge between Ongiva and Mongua on the hard-surfaced road, thereby denying access to any more supplies getting to FAPLA (Popular Front for the Liberation of Angola) and SWAPO bases; to engage and destroy any convoys coming down the road, capture any enemy equipment and recover any bodies of foreign personnel – Russians or Cubans. We were to use UNITA forces inside Angola as our guides.

The raiding force consisted of five vehicles: two Jackals with twin 7.62mm MAG machine guns for the gunner and his assistant, and one machine gun for the co-driver; one 2½-ton vehicle with a 14.5mm heavy machine gun captured from SWAPO; and two 2½-ton vehicles to carry troops and demolition equipment with one mounted 7.62 MAG. There were 12 of us from the Pathfinders and we were assisted by eight members of 1 Parachute Brigade fire force (Parabats) who were also based in Ondangwa.

As soon as all equipment and personnel were ready we began organising and rehearsing to destroy the bridge culvert and any convoy we encountered. Current intelligence reports and aerial photos were obtained to study and organise appropriate equipment to destroy the bridge. We intended to use approximately 400 pounds of explosives and supports had to be prepared to keep the explosives tight against the culvert roof. We improvised and made metal supports to hold the explosives in place against the roof of the culvert. The latest intelligence reports said convoy movements were currently between midnight and 5am because of constant SAAF attacks, rendering daylight travel for FAPLA and SWAPO impossible.

During a three-day rehearsal on the nearby Etosha Pan we practised battle formations. First in the convoy was the first Jackal vehicle; then one Unimog 2½-ton truck carrying UNITA guides and Para personnel; next was the other 2½-ton Unimog with the explosives and other equipment; then another Unimog with its 14.5mm heavy machine gun; and in the final position was another Jackal vehicle. We repeatedly practised the actions we would take once we reached the bridge. Potential mistakes were corrected, and again and again we went over the command and control elements to ensure that operation would go smoothly.

The key part of the raid was to ensure that the culvert was blown with as many enemy vehicles on it as possible – this required good communications between the various ambush groups. After three intense days and nights I felt that every man knew his job and what he was expected to do. We packed the vehicles and moved to an SADF base at just south of the border with Angola. The next day we moved to a large UNITA base camp some 18 miles inside Angola. The UNITA soldiers had their families with them and were very curious about us and our equipment. They asked many questions and were obviously puzzled as to why the majority of our group could not speak Afrikaans. There were some advisers with UNITA who had been with the Portuguese Army during the 1975 war and were now fighting for UNITA. The children of the camp crowded around our vehicles and especially the Jackals. Disturbingly some 80 per cent of the male children above ten years old carried weapons, the majority of which were the Hungarian-type AK-47s with folding butts or the Spanish-made 7.62mm CETME rifle. There were a number of captured AK-47s and AKMs and a few officers had Russian Tokorov pistols.

The next morning, I gave a final briefing and we pored over maps and aerial photographs of the target area. We still had 75 miles to travel, primarily through SWAPO/FAPLA-controlled territory, but with UNITA guides we hoped to avoid most of the enemy's base camps. Later that night at about 10pm while travelling through the bush, a mopane tree stump ripped the fuel tank off one of the support Unimogs. As we tried to repair the vehicle by shaded torchlight noise became a serious problem. Each village seemed to have a guard system and the noise we were making had obviously alerted them to something happening. They communicated between *kraals* by firing shots into the air with their old Mausers. I decided we should masquerade as FAPLA soldiers by singing and turning on all the vehicle lights, making as much noise as possible. Hopefully we could bluff our way past these home guards. The ruse worked and the shots stopped! At 3am we had completed the repairs and got out of there as quickly as possible. We reached the main asphalt road deliberately north of our destination and then moved south-east to locate the bridge. I sent the two Jackals up and down the road as early warning and as stop-groups once the ambush was triggered. At the culvert we had to work fast because of the delay we had suffered. The demolitions team started unloading and setting up the demolitions assisted by the Parabats. The demolition preparation was very slick due to our many rehearsals and only took about 30 minutes. We used about 440 pounds of PE/C4 and Mike L, one of the demolition team and a former US Special Forces operator, considered it was about five times more than we needed. But what the hell – using the old demolitionists' expression, 'P for plenty!' and why not. Then came the wait and by 4am it was very, very cold.

My plan was to wait until 5am to blow the bridge and move back to friendly lines. Unfortunately, no convoy came by. We blew the culvert and the tar-sealed road. KFB! It was an impressive sight and sound with dirt and concrete scattered over some 600 yards leaving a crater the size of a large bus. We placed booby-traps around the area using captured Russian landmines and mechanical claymore ambushes. We then moved directly towards friendly lines, even if it meant going through enemy-controlled areas. Occasionally, we stopped and laid more booby-traps and, at one stage, we spotted enemy troops trailing us and opened fire with the 14.5mm heavy machine gun. They quickly disappeared.

After about an hour's driving one of the Unimogs drove into a concealed crater. The crater was almost the exact size of the truck itself! This presented the major problem of trying to extract the vehicle due to its tight fit inside the crater. While we were working out how to pull the vehicle out we heard the ominous rumblings of tracked and other armoured vehicles. We knew that FAPLA soldiers were now looking for us. We had few anti-tank weapons – only several RPG-7s – so a fight with armoured vehicles was not a good idea. I advised Sector 10 headquarters at Oshikati of our situation, but I was not very confident that support for us would be forthcoming. I particularly requested air support to deter the armoured vehicles. This was denied by Sector 10. To this day, I believe it was because we were expendable – after all we were mostly *uitlanders* (foreigners).

Fortunately, and maybe it was the incentive of the armoured vehicles closing in, we were finally able to literally jerk the Unimog out of the ground using a flexible tow-rope. By now the closest enemy vehicle was not much more than half a mile away and closing in on us. They had obviously worked out that we would be moving south. However, they were moving very cautiously as a result of the mines we had laid so we were able to gain some space. After a further two hours driving we re-entered UNITA-controlled territory. I gave the UNITA officers a quick brief on our task and we then re-crossed the border into South West Africa and returned to our base in Ondangwa.

The following day I briefed Sector 10 headquarters staff at Oshikati on the raid and later they were able to provide additional information about the interdiction of the main road we had caused.

There were other moments of excitement during my time with the SADF – some that I certainly had not expected. On 18 May 1981 I was in South West Africa in the base camp of the Parabats sitting in the operations room. I was doing some operational planning with Sergeant Major Dennis Croukamp. Sergeant Major Croukamp had served with the Rhodesian Light Infantry, and had been awarded one of the earliest Bronze Cross of Rhodesia gallantry awards for bravery under fire. He had then served with the Selous Scouts. He had a great operational reputation. At approximately 9pm, Sergeant Kevin O'Connor, a Rhodesian, who was one of the administration members of the Pathfinders in a quartermaster capacity, burst into the room. He fired a single shot and then a burst of three to four rounds into the wall above our heads. The operations room was a sandbagged tent with a canvas roof. I had my back to the door and stood up to face Sergeant O'Connor. He was carrying an R4 assault rifle with a 50-round magazine attached and wearing chest webbing containing a further six magazines and also a 9mm pistol with two magazines. He was in an extremely agitated state and said words to the effect that he was going to sort out Croukamp once and for all, after which he fired another burst into the wall. He then ordered Croukamp to sit opposite him and covered him with his loaded weapon with the safety catch off. It subsequently came to light that Croukamp and O'Connor had been involved in an altercation earlier in the day.

I asked O'Connor if I could go outside and let the camp know what was happening because there would have been some confusion concerning the source of the firing, which could indicate that we were undergoing a ground attack. He agreed and ordered me to ring the brigade commander and tell him he wanted the brigade commander to come and see him or he would shoot Croukamp. I went outside, briefed the senior Para officer present, gave a quick outline of the situation and organised some contingency plans in case matters deteriorated. One of the plans involved setting up a 7.62mm MAG on a tripod outside the operations room directly in line with O'Connor.

O'Connor was still very agitated and had placed Croukamp opposite the operations room door, so he could shoot him and anyone attempting to gain entry through the door. I persuaded him to put Croukamp on the far side of the room, ostensibly to protect the signaller in the adjacent room who had been fearlessly carrying on his duties with this mayhem going on outside his cubicle. The other reason that I wanted him to move was to increase the area that O'Connor would have to watch giving me further options at a later time. My main task was to calm O'Connor, so that he would become more predictable and would not be impulsive. I did this by talking to him, discussing miscellaneous subjects, and generally defusing the situation.

I then persuaded him to put on the safety of his weapon for all our security. He did so for a few minutes but because it was difficult to remove quickly he returned the safety catch to automatic. He complained of a headache, so I obtained some aspirin for him; he was very wary, but took them and also some soft drinks. I was able to slowly win his confidence and as a result was permitted to move to and from the room and therefore at intervals I could brief others outside of the situation. I frequently attempted to persuade O'Connor to release Croukamp and use me as a hostage instead. I considered that he was unlikely to injure me. However, he refused each time. I was also attempting to make him give me the R4 as a sign of his willingness to surrender when the brigade commander arrived. The R4 has a very fast rate of fire and was a source of much danger to everyone in the vicinity.

I was concerned that the generator providing the light for the camp might accidentally fail, which could make O'Connor open fire, so I convinced him to allow me to get a gas lamp. Each time I moved O'Connor always kept Croukamp covered and did not provide me with an opportunity to overpower him without danger to Croukamp.

At approximately 11.15pm O'Connor suddenly became very agitated. He had calmed down over the course of the preceding two hours, but he threatened to take Croukamp 'off at the knees'. The situation was deteriorating rapidly, and I made greater efforts to take O'Connor's mind off the current situation. I convinced him that the only way the brigadier would come into the room would be if I took the R4 outside first to clearly show that he had no intention of harming the brigadier. He finally agreed to this.

At approximately 11.45pm I was told that the brigadier had arrived and requested that O'Connor give me the R4 as discussed. He had already cocked his pistol and removed the safety catch from 'safe' during one of my earlier absences. He slowly stood up, unloaded the R4, and with the pistol in one hand pushed the R4 across the bench seat towards me. I moved to pick it up and was at last able to get close to him. I pushed him off balance with the R4 and then after a struggle overpowered him and removed the pistol from him. Although still shocked, Croukamp was able to assist me in the struggle.

There was a moment when I could have shot O'Connor with his own pistol but reinforcements had arrived and O'Connor was handcuffed and led away. Once I was sure the situation was under control I had a cup of coffee and retired to my tent.

Surprisingly, within a few days, O'Connor was sent unescorted back to his military quarters where he lived with his family to arrange his defence in his forthcoming court martial. Unsurprisingly, he fled the country instead and went to the UK. Dennis Croukamp has written a book about his military experiences and in my copy of his book he has kindly written 'Thank you for saving my life'.

As well as commanding the Brigade Pathfinders on operation, alternating with Colonel Breytenbach I was responsible for coordinating training in South Africa for the non-permanent force members of 2 and 3 Para battalions. 1 Parachute Battalion was the Para training battalion for conscripts and was based in Tempe, near Bloemfontein. 2 and 3 Battalions were Paras who had completed their two-year compulsory military training including border operations and were now serving in the Citizen Force (CF) of fully trained but part-time reservists. This often included further operational service. I was very impressed by the way the call-up for this training was conducted. There were very few permanent force staff in the Para battalions and the annual training almost appeared ad hoc but was in fact very well organised despite the fact that there was little formal training during the year. This was a legacy of the Boer War and similar to how the Boer Commandos operated. I was also interested to note that parachute dispatching was carried out by the Paras themselves and not by SAAF personnel. Normally, in my experience, an air force jealously guards its involvement in military parachuting and army Paras are normally only 'assistant' parachute jump instructors. I umpired a training airborne assault with 3 Battalion into Zululand. We parachuted from a fleet of SAAF Transalls, baby Hercules. The Paras carried their R4s strapped to their sides, wearing all their webbing equipment with their versatile chest webbing for ammunition magazines and grenades. We dropped from a height of approximately 600 feet onto a thorn bush-covered DZ. Other Paras I have jumped with outside the SADF are deathly quiet on take-off and pre-occupied with their own thoughts and fears. Not the SADF Paras – they stamped their feet and clapped their hands in unison – bang, bang, bang on the floor, clapping and shouting 'Let's go!' until the aircraft left the ground. That was a bit different!

I also ran training courses for 'new' Pathfinders before they deployed with the rest of the Pathfinder Company. One of the training courses I ran for the Pathfinders was a Resistance to Interrogation course. This involved putting Pathfinders under mild physical and mental pressure through the use of blindfolds, isolation in shallow pits surrounded by bits of meat to attract irritating flies, and silence. The soldiers were interrogated using very basic 'good guy versus bad guy' techniques but with no physical violence whatsoever. This was to prepare the Pathfinders for the unlikely event of capture by the enemy. They were to repeat the mantra of number, rank, name and date of birth only. I ran the course in the Caprivi Strip and we were based at the SADF Special Forces base at Fort Doppies. The Special Forces operators at Fort Doppies had a tame lion called Terry which they had reared from a cub. Terry was very friendly and would wander around the camp and the local area. During the resistance to interrogation course, one of the support staff had gone into the bush to answer the call of nature and, suddenly, came running back into the camp with his trousers around his ankles shouting in Afrikaans, 'A fucking lion! A fucking lion!' Trotting calmly along behind him was Terry.

A few days later I was giving a lecture; this was done in the open air sitting on the ground, when in padded Terry who proceeded to sit on the lap of a very, very startled Pathfinder. Terry listened to the lecture for a few minutes and then wandered away again. On another occasion when Terry had not been seen for a while some troops from Fort Doppies went out in a Buffel to drop off some meat for him. They eventually found a lion and one of the soldiers climbed out with the meat and carried it over. He would have made the South African Olympic track team with the speed with which he returned to the vehicle when his companion said, 'Here's Terry – beside the Buffel!' Walking up to a wild lion with an armful of raw meat is certainly not a recommended activity.

Several years later as the SADF was leaving the border area it was decided to take Terry to a game reserve in the south of South Africa. A cage was duly built and a Dakota flew into the nearby bush airstrip to take Terry to his new home. Unfortunately, the new cage was too big to fit through the doors of the Dakota. Rather than cancel the flight and build a new cage the operators at the Fort simply informed the pilot that they would drug Terry and put him in the back of the plane. Apparently, the pilot's face was a picture as he looked at Terry in his cage and said, 'If you think I am flying my plane with a fucking great lion sleeping in the back you have to be out of your fucking heads!' He then climbed back into his plane and left. Some weeks later Terry went south in a smaller cage and, I hope, lived happily ever after in his new home.

In mid-July 1981 I was tasked with deploying with the Brigade Pathfinders in Ondangwa to operate above the 'cut line' north of Ombalantu to carry out multiple foot patrols in Angola in a block patrol area 19 miles east of the Cunane River and for 19 miles north into Angola. I briefed the company on our task and we travelled in Buffel APCs along the 'black top' past Oshikati, the SADF sector headquarters, to Ombalantu where we turned north to a specific border marker on the 'cut line' marking the border between SWA Owambo Province and Angola. We left the Buffels and their escort to return to Ondangwa and patrolled in open formation north towards an old Portuguese dam that I had designated as the centre of our patrol area. We reached an area 200 yards short of the dam at about 4.30am. Despite the difficulties of night navigation for 15 miles in a featureless terrain my navigation was accurate. After resting for several hours I deployed three eight-man patrols to pre-designated areas to the west, north and east of my headquarters group. They were to carry out patrols looking for enemy signs. At 9pm on the second night the northern patrol observed a four-man SWAPO group approaching a nearby well. The patrol engaged them, killing one and dispersing the others. A sweep of the contact area was carried out the following morning but did not locate any further enemy casualties, only several blood trails. As the patrol was preparing to move to a new location,

Dave Barr moved to a small bush to answer the call of nature and nearly trod on an equally surprised SWAPO soldier lying in the grass. He immediately raced back to the patrol position, alerting his comrades. The patrol position was then heavily engaged, with small arms fire, RPG 7 rockets, and 60mm mortar bombs landing near the patrol position. The patrol immediately returned fire and prepared to make a tactical withdrawal and break contact with the enemy. As soon as we heard the contact my headquarters patrol started moving north towards the contact area as did the other two patrols. I linked up with the withdrawing patrol as well as the two other patrols and, now consolidated, we swept back north to the contact area. Using fire and movement we entered the area of the contact but SWAPO had left. We observed a number of blood trails and spent AK-47 and RPD machine gun cases. We continued sweeping the area and located a recently occupied enemy temporary base camp with trenches. This was why the enemy had been able to mount an attack in such a short time. After thoroughly checking the area we moved south-west towards the border and established a firm base for further patrolling. Later SADF sigint (signals intelligence) advised us that 30–40 SWAPO had been involved in this firefight.

On a lighter note, just before dawn on the morning after we had redeployed I was most surprised to hear the sound of 'Yankee Doodle' being played by someone's watch. The owner had obviously forgotten to mute it. From the tune it was obviously one of our US colleagues. There were assorted chuckles from the surrounding night perimeter. If there had been any SWAPO in the area they would certainly have been as bemused as we were to hear this music in the pre-dawn silence of the veldt.

We continued patrolling without success but several days later I was recalled to Army HQ in Pretoria regarding my service contract with the SADF. I was escorted by one of the patrols back to the 'cut line' to rendezvous with a patrol of Buffels and returned to our base in Ondangwa. The company continued patrolling for another two weeks but without any contacts. The following day I flew from Ondangwa by C-130 to Waterkloof SAAF base in Pretoria. Sadly, this was to be my last operation with the Brigade Pathfinders, 'The Philistines', as I was soon to leave the SADF.

Meanwhile, from 24 August to 4 September 1981 the Pathfinders and their Jackals were heavily involved in the major SADF Operation *Protea* in which up to 5,000 SADF soldiers occupied Cunene Province in Southern Angola.

South Africa was not to be home to me for much longer. After just under a year in the SADF I regretfully handed in my resignation. The SADF was not prepared to fulfil the financial terms of my initial contract and so my young family and I were unable to remain. As the Pathfinders were deployed on Operation *Protea* at the time I was sadly unable to bid my 'universal soldier' comrades a proper farewell. Colonel Breytenbach himself was soon to leave the unit he had created. In the latter half of 1982 the colonel was posted out of 44 Brigade and many of the original Pathfinders decided to leave the SADF as a result. Jan Breytenbach had been responsible for setting up and establishing all of the SADF Special Forces, as well as the formidable 32 Battalion, and was an individual of immense personal courage and determination. He was not one to be bothered by military minutiae – that was the job of staff officers. He had great imagination and really understood the immense value of well-trained small groups of men carrying out strategic operations against far larger numbers. However, to a number of straight-laced Boer career officers in the SADF he was an anathema, a maverick, and those who worked with him also fell under this shadow. I am very proud to have served with him – and the Parabats.

A new future now beckoned.

7

KMS LIMITED, 1982 AND 21 SAS

I had two options when I left South Africa. One was a three-year short-term engagement as training officer at 22 SAS and the other was to join David W at KMS, a private military company (PMC) based in London. Initially KMS had more to offer in the long term than rejoining the British Army so I accepted their offer. I had a few months between leaving the SADF and joining KMS so my family and I returned to New Zealand and we stayed with relatives in Christchurch. I took a job as a wool packer at a warehouse in Christchurch and Cecilia worked as a chambermaid at one of the large hotels. We needed the money.

I must admit that wool packing is one of the hardest physical jobs I have ever had. Wool packing involves packing wool into large hessian bags; compressing the wool on a press; weighing the bag; and then sewing it up. It may sound relatively simple to do but it was physically extremely demanding. I was relieved when the New Year dawned and I could set off to London to join KMS in January 1982.

KMS had been set up by Major David W, a former 22 SAS squadron commander, and it provided security services to a number of eminent people. I was to meet several famous and powerful people while working for KMS. These included the Aga Khan; Sheikh Yamani, the Saudi oil minister; and David Stirling, the founder of the British SAS. The company also provided logistical support for the Sultan of Oman's Special Forces (SSF), which was based in Dhofar Province in the south of Oman. This logistics support comprised everything that SSF could need from pencils to machine guns, Land Rovers and boats. KMS also recruited all the European officers and some senior NCOs for this Special Force regiment. There was certainly never a dull moment while I worked with KMS.

I went on a management visit to one of the close protection teams looking after Sheikh Yamani at his villa in Sardinia. Being a close protection officer is certainly an interesting way of life, but you can only provide the level of protection that the client wants. Sheikh Yamani was the Saudi oil minister from 1962 to 1986 and during that time he had survived kidnapping by Carlos 'The Jackal' at an OPEC conference on 21 December 1975 in Vienna, Austria. His close protection team was very professional and was composed of former members of British Special Forces. At the time of my visit he had hired a small and discreet car. Blending into the environment was certainly a sensible decision; however, as the car was only two-door this meant that the two armed bodyguards sat in the back of the car while the Sheikh and his wife sat in the front. I was never quite sure how the protection team was going to be able to do anything in the event of an incident.

Another key task I had was to liaise with the Sultan of Oman's Special Force in Dhofar and I spent a number of weeks with them on a series of separate visits. This special force was composed mainly of Jebalis, the mountain people from Dhofar. A number of these Jebalis had been the enemy, or *Adoo*, during the communist-inspired insurgency against Sultan Qaboos and his father before him. Most of the senior officers in the regiment were former British Special Forces and, subsequently, a few also came from the Rhodesian Special Forces. But the intention was to eventually replace all the British staff with Omanis.

The night skies in the deserts of Oman were stunning. It was reminiscent of the nights I had enjoyed under African skies just the year before, with the reassuring presence of the Southern Cross. I loved any time I could get out in the wilderness. In spite of these exotic travels with KMS, I also spent a lot of time visiting clients in London and various other European cities.

THE CHELSEA CHINDITS

It was while I was with KMS that I decided to join 21 SAS, the reserve branch of the SAS, headquartered in the Kings Road in London, and nicknamed the 'Chelsea Chindits'. I was in good company; Jim J a director at KMS, was a former CO of 21 SAS. I was told by Tony L, the CO, that I would have to pass selection again. This was a bit strange as he had been my squadron commander in 22 SAS. However, this was at a time when Special Forces Headquarters was concerned about the number of SAS personnel leaving the British Army to work on lucrative security contracts and well before the days of 'Special Forces' pay.

I spent about a year in 21 SAS as A Squadron commander, and went on annual camp with the regiment to Germany. Even though I was the squadron commander I went out as a standard patrol member in order to learn more about the regiment's proposed wartime role. In those days 21 and 23 SAS were the corps patrol units (CPU) and in the event of hostilities, or hopefully prior to hostilities, they would dig hides on the north German plains to observe likely Soviet armoured invasion routes. These hides would monitor the Soviet troop movements and direct conventional weapons or tactical nuclear weapons on to key headquarters and communications groups.

On this annual camp we lived in a hole in the ground which we dug out by hand, the traditional way. Conditions were appalling with four people living 6-foot underground, in a T-shaped hole, with only a small plastic pipe to the surface for ventilation. We had plastic bags to crap into and bottles in which to urinate. At one end of the hole was a burning candle. We had to monitor the candle in case it went out which meant the air had become too foul to breathe and a small air pump was then activated. A coal-mine canary would soon have keeled over in one of our hides.

One man in the hole observed our area of responsibility through a periscope while the others tried to sleep between shifts or send signal situation reports to the corps headquarters. It was a very, very grim existence indeed!

One of the vulnerabilities of the hides was the very restricted ability to observe what was happening on the surface above the hide. The periscope had limited traverse as its primary aim was to observe only certain arcs. One weekend, prior to the annual camp, we had a presentation by some 'spooks' from the intelligence services who had designed a listening device which could be used from our underground hides. With great flair and enthusiasm, they presented their 'listening device' to the gathered SAS operators. The device was a giant pair of green human-shaped ears which were to be attached to a tree and the cables would run into the hide. There was a stunned silence from the assembled group and this was followed by gales of laughter. The 'spooks' were deeply hurt, gathered up their 'ears', and quickly departed.

The personal hygiene of one particular patrol member in our hide left a lot to be desired before we even dug the hole. He was even more fragrant after several days in the hole and, by the second day, the whole team was wearing gas masks! I suspect that in a real war situation, after three weeks in this hole being nuked by the Soviets would have come as welcome relief.

Overall, it was an interesting concept but very much a suicide mission. Nowadays, technology has made such measures obsolete.

This was my first real introduction to working closely with the Territorial Army (TA). They were not generally respected by the regular army who called them STABs (stupid TA bastards) and the TA responded in kind by calling regular army soldiers ARABs (arrogant regular army bastards). However, I was very impressed with the commitment and enthusiasm of the TA soldier. Having worked a full week, often on night shifts, they would parade on a Friday night in their TA Centre and be away on exercise until late Sunday afternoon, before starting work again on a Monday. In many ways this could be much harder graft than the regular army was experiencing.

The TA is managed by permanent cadres from the regular army and this was also the case with the reserve SAS. Officers and senior NCOs from 22 SAS were posted to each TA SAS unit for two to three years. The commanding officer would be either TA or regular with the second-in-command, adjutant and regimental sergeant major all being regulars.

Each sub-unit would also have a small cadre of regular 22 SAS soldiers. The majority of the cadre staff were good value but there were a few who had little time for the TA and spent most of their time and effort maximising the various allowances that attachment to the TA provided. This was a shame as it partially eroded the high regard the reserves had for the regular SAS.

I worked with KMS for some 12 months and then David W asked if I would go to Oman to serve with the Sultan's Special Forces on a contract for several years. This was an unaccompanied position and it would have meant more long absences from my young family. This was not a situation I wanted at that time and so I decided to see if I could re-enlist in the New Zealand Army instead. I was accepted and once I had completed the formalities in London I received a posting as training officer of the New Zealand SAS. I was very excited about this new challenge and so KMS and I amicably parted company and my family and I prepared to return to New Zealand, which we had left some seven years previously.

8

NEW ZEALAND ARMY, 1982–85

Just prior to leaving for New Zealand my posting was abruptly changed to that of adjutant of the Army Schools in Waiouru. An adjutant is essentially a personal staff officer for a unit commander. I was very disappointed by this late change but I was now committed to returning to New Zealand so there was not much I could do. This was a captain's appointment whereas I had been a substantive major in the British Army. Moreover, I was to lose some six years seniority with my New Zealand Army peers. There were obviously a number within the army who felt I had been disloyal by previously leaving and this was my punishment. The fact that I now probably had more operational experience than any other officer in the New Zealand Army as well as having attended military courses in the United Kingdom that New Zealand officers were most unlikely to be selected for, was ignored. This reminded me, if I needed reminding, of how parochial the New Zealand Army could be.

But, by this point, I was fully committed and duly took up my appointment in Waiouru. It was certainly an interesting situation because, despite being of a more junior rank to the officers I worked with, I had known them all as snotty little officer cadets or subalterns from my earlier years in the New Zealand Army. A number had delusions of grandeur, but this carried little weight with me as I knew their foibles from long before.

I was reminded of the vagaries of life during an incident in Waiouru. While attending a senior staff officer course we were perched on a hill carrying out a Tactical Exercise Without Troops (TEWT). This is a military exercise where officers are given various tactical problems to solve against a fictitious enemy which was, in our case, the 'Musorians', a mythical force loosely based upon the Indonesian Army against whom we deployed our own mythical troops. The exercise involved us walking the area concerned in order to decide where we would place our troops, weapons and any supporting elements such as tanks and artillery.

On this particular day we were supported by an Army Air Corps Sioux helicopter piloted by Captain Pete Speedie. It would take two officers at a time to look around the area of the exercise. The Sioux buzzed in and out with its passengers while the rest of us studied maps and wrote our plans. Suddenly, I detected an unusual note in the noise of the helicopter and looked up. To my horror I saw it was descending at great speed. I could see it was going to land very, very heavily. The helicopter smashed into the ground, bounced into the air and then crashed down again. As it hit the second time the exterior fuel tanks fell away, the tail structure bent and broke and the Plexiglas bubble shattered. The three occupants were lying limply inside. My colleagues and I rushed over to the wreckage and, as we saw flames, removed the casualties from the wreckage and took them a safe distance away before examining them for injuries. They were all suffering from impact trauma and, as a Special Forces trained medic, I carried out injury checks. One of the occupants was unable to feel his legs and I suspected a serious injury to his spine. We immobilised him and the others as best we could and by this time an ambulance had arrived from Waiouru Camp. The injured were all taken to the base hospital there. Two of the occupants recovered and the pilot was able to continue flying but sadly the third occupant, Phil Blundell, was permanently injured and is a paraplegic. He continued in the New Zealand Army and was a very successful senior logistics officer for many years.

The Sioux is designed to break up on impact thereby dissipating the shock of a hard landing on its passengers. The two outside seats are designed to fold and bend in a crash but the passenger in the centre seat is on a rigid part of the aircraft and there is little or no give in his seat at all. This is where Phil had been sitting.

───────

As a family we really enjoyed living in Waiouru. It is situated on the volcanic plateau in the centre of the North Island and the environment has dramatic, vast rolling tussock-covered plains dominated by the imposing mountain collection of Ruapehu, Tongariro and the active volcano Ngarahoe. The New Zealand Army family housing, as always, was spartan and houses were completely unfurnished with the only heating coming from a 'chippy' stove located, for some reason, behind the kitchen door. It was bitterly cold in winter when there was always snow on the ground.

It certainly hadn't been the job I had wanted but I was fortunate in that I had a decent commanding officer in Lieutenant Colonel Graham Talbot, a very efficient and good-natured Corps of Transportation officer. One day the CO was in his office reprimanding a young officer for some minor infraction. The reprimand complete, the officer saluted and marched smartly into the nearby broom cupboard. Much to his credit he remained inside the cupboard until we had vacated the office.

My luck held as my next CO was Lieutenant Colonel Neil 'Nail' Bradley, an engineering officer, who, like me, had previously completed an operational tour of Vietnam – he had been with the NZ Artillery there. Immediately prior to this new appointment he had spent time attached to a US Army school of instruction and was now a complete zealot, committed to reorganising the training philosophy of the New Zealand Army schools. It was good to have such a serious task to sink our teeth into and we got along well.

I did well in my new appointment and was soon promoted to major and then, following good grades on the promotion courses, I was selected to attend the New Zealand Command and Staff College. This gave me a great deal of personal satisfaction because I had previously decided not to take up the opportunity to attend the prestigious British Staff College in Camberley where I had been selected as a 'direct entry' candidate.

The New Zealand Joint Services Staff College was situated in the Royal New Zealand Air Force (RNZAF) base at Whenuapai, north of Auckland, and was very much an RNZAF-controlled staff college with little joint military education carried out. We learned, amongst other things, all about the various bomb loads of antiquated New Zealand aircraft and the turn-around times for a strike on Indonesia's air force bases from Changi airbase in Singapore. The course took the best part of a year and I graduated in December 1984. The most useful part of the course was working and discussing military and political matters with my fellow students including a fellow infantry officer, Major Rob 'Shorty' Hughes, and Major Keith Rawlings of the Royal New Zealand Army Service Corps. At the end of the course it was very satisfying to be able to use the title 'psc' (passed staff college) but I still cannot tell you what is the bomb load of a Canberra bomber or the loiter-over-target time for a Skyhawk!

In January 1985, after two years in Waiouru I was posted as the second-in-command of the 2/1st Royal New Zealand Infantry Battalion in Burnham. This unit had been called the 1st Battalion Depot for many years and it was where I had completed my infantry soldier training and where I had been based prior to travelling overseas to join 1 RNZIR in Singapore in 1969. With the permanent return of 1 RNZIR, a name change took place, and it officially became the 2/1st Royal New Zealand Infantry Battalion. I obviously knew Burnham well and it was great to be back working with Kiwi infantry soldiers once again. I also had the pleasure of working closely with 'Shorty' Hughes, my classmate at Staff College.

But as much as I enjoyed the day-to-day challenges of my role, it also became increasingly obvious to me that I had limited further promotion opportunities. I had reached the top rung of the ladder, not due to my abilities, but because I had obviously committed a sin of disloyalty by having previously left to pursue overseas opportunities. The New Zealand Army was, and still is, small and insular and the careers of officers could be permanently affected by the subjective views and comments of a single more senior officer. The British Army had been too large for personality clashes to permanently affect an officer's career but here in New Zealand it was a different matter. I was not aware of having any particular 'enemies' within the system but I did realise that there were a number of officers who were resentful and envious of my military travels.

I had been contacted by the newly appointed CO of the Sultan of Oman's Special Forces, Keith F, with whom I had worked when still part of KMS, offering me an appointment. This was certainly a more challenging prospect than what was on offer with the New Zealand Army so on completion of my three-year contract I submitted my resignation from the New Zealand Army for a second time.

There was some ill-feeling amongst a number of senior officers when I did this but, considering their generally appalling officer management, was I really expected to stay and become a tired, boring, passed-over major – I don't think so! Besides, there was very little operational experience to be gained if I remained with the New Zealand Army. Odin was calling, it was time to get back in the thick of it.

9

THE SULTAN OF OMAN'S SPECIAL FORCES, 1985-89

I previously had first-hand dealings with the Sultan of Oman's Special Forces (SSF) when I was working with KMS in London. The recently appointed commanding officer was Keith F whom I had known well during my time in both the British SAS and the Parachute Regiment. I was made an offer of a three-year contract with the SSF as commander of D Squadron, the counterterrorism squadron and, soon after, this appointment also included being the regimental second-in-command.

The regiment was and still is based at Zeak, on the top of the mountain escarpment on a large plateau. The mountains of Jebel Dhofar, which rise to 3,000 feet, encircle the Salalah plain and stretch westwards into Yemen. The rugged terrain makes communications very difficult and the population remains dominated by isolated communities of tribesmen.

The SSF was composed of mountain people from the Dhofar, the southern region of Oman, and these Jebalis (*jebel* means 'mountain' in Arabic) were fierce, loyal and independent leading a nomadic existence in the mountains between Salalah and the Yemen.

The Dhofaris, including the Jebalis, had been a source of irritation to Sultan Said bin Taimur, the absolute ruler and father of the present sultan, Qaboos bin Said. He ensured that very little money was invested in the area or its infrastructure. Oman had oil money, but the sultan was a reactionary and was quite happy for Oman to remain in the dark ages even though neighbouring countries such as the United Arab Emirates were investing in the education of their citizens and the modernisation of their countries.

Following the British withdrawal from Aden and the Yemen, communist factions fomented an insurrection amongst the Yemeni people and this crossed across into Dhofar. A bloody rebellion against Sultan Said bin Taimur was started in the Dhofar region in 1962 and this continued until 1976. The Sultan utilised Baluchi soldiers from southern India, British Army training teams and an Iranian brigade as well as Oman's own limited military resources to try to quell the rebellion. On 23 July 1970 the present sultan, Sultan Qaboos, overthrew his father in a virtually bloodless coup. His father banished himself to the Savoy hotel in London where he stayed until he died in 1972.

Sultan Qaboos took a completely different view from his father and knew that financial investment and modernisation were the keys to peace in the southern provinces. Moreover, by pursuing these aims, he removed the main sources of disaffection amongst the Dhofaris, which had been promoted by their Marxist Yemeni agitators. In 1976 the Dhofar War, as it was known, was declared over; however, there remained a number of armed and well-trained Jebalis who, despite receiving financial assistance and weapon amnesties, could become a source of potential discontent within the region. These Jebalis who had been former enemy, or *Adoo*, as well as other Jebalis were recruited into a new unit called the Sultan of Oman's Special Force (SSF). SSF was managed logistically by KMS Limited in London. It was a massive and, of course, lucrative undertaking.

The first commander of SSF was Alan 'Ram' S, a Royal Marine, former commander of the Special Boat Service (SBS) and a recipient of the Military Cross. A new commanding officer was sought when he left the unit and, in the interim, Andrew N commanded the unit. Andrew N was a former Intelligence Corps officer who had served in the intelligence cell at 22 SAS in Hereford and then with the Director of Special Forces in London. After leaving the army he joined KMS. I had replaced him in KMS in London when he went out to Oman. The designated commanding officer was

Julian 'Tony' B, MBE MC, with whom I had served in 22 SAS. Sadly, while they were together in Oman during their handover both Tony and Andrew N were killed on 2 May 1981 when the Range Rover in which they were travelling overturned near the Oman Air Force base in Thumrait, Dhofar.

The post of commander of the SSF was filled by Keith F – an interesting character. I knew him from when he was second-in-command of 22 SAS and he was also a former Parachute Regiment officer. He was very much a go-getter. He wasn't destined to command a regular SAS regiment, but he had commanded 21 SAS. He had an unusual background for an officer, having joined the army later in life after having first been a cub reporter for a northern newspaper.

Following Keith's offer, I officially joined the SSF in 1985. Unfortunately, it was an unaccompanied posting and the terms of service were three months' duty, followed by a month of leave. I did miss my wife and family and some three years of my two children growing up. I hope I was able to make up for my absences by the holidays we were able to have when we were all together during my leave periods.

The main base at Zeak was centrally placed for nearly all the tribes in the area. There was another smaller camp in the north of Oman near the international airport at Seeb. Some years later a second SSF regiment was created and based in this other camp.

The soldiers, NCOs and junior officers of the regiment were all Jebalis while the senior officers were former British officers and senior NCOs, the majority of whom had served in the British SAS. British officers of the Sultan's Armed Forces (SAF) Baluchi Battalions, who still provided many of the Omani forces, would disparagingly call the SSF 'The Corporals on the Hill', because of the number of former 22 SAS NCOs who were now officers in the unit.

Ironically, a number of members of the regiment had been on opposite sides during the Dhofar War and this led to many interesting discussions as the older Jebalis and the SAS soldiers would compare various actions in which they had both participated throughout the mountains.

Working alongside me at SSF Headquarters was the late Captain Tony F MBE. Tony had also been a senior NCO in 22 SAS and had been seriously injured in a contact in September 1975 with the *Adoo* while serving in Oman. The incident left him wheelchair-bound but despite his very serious injuries he attended Cairo University and was a fluent Arabist. He was also an expert in all the various Dhofari tribes and their families. Despite the paralysis of his lower limbs he was fiercely independent and did not let his mobility issues get him down. He had a suitably converted car and would often drive himself the 620 miles between Muscat, the capital of Oman, and Salalah, the capital of Dhofar Province, on his own. He was highly respected by everyone in the SSF and was awarded an MBE in 1987. Sadly, in 1994, he succumbed to his injuries, several years after he had left the SSF.

The SSF was, as would be expected, very well resourced and financed. Its equipment and facilities were of the highest order. The uniform was either green Dacron or camouflage topped by a beret of imperial purple – the personal colour choice of Sultan Qaboos. One of the regiment's nicknames was 'The Lavender Hill Mob'.

The unit had three 'Sabre' (fighting) squadrons, which were highly mobile and based on desert Land Rovers, and a counterterrorism squadron. All operational members of the unit were para trained and parachute drops were frequently carried out from Oman Air Force (SOAF) aircraft, mainly Skyvans.

After I had been with the SSF a while I was able to convince Keith F that he should look elsewhere for suitably qualified officers rather than simply from within British Special Forces. He agreed, and we were subsequently joined by some excellent former Rhodesian Army officers and an Australian Vietnam veteran as well as two other New Zealanders. To a man they were all very professional officers and more widely experienced than the former SAS SSF officers, most of whom had been other ranks in the SAS. The former Rhodesian Army officers, in particular, had a great deal of recent combat experience and this was most useful in developing operational procedures for the SSF. We had a Rhodesian Army signals officer and officers from the Selous Scouts and the Rhodesian SAS.

The New Zealanders were Keith Rawlings, who had been at Staff College with me and commanded the SSF Headquarters Company, and Ron Mark, who was a former New Zealand officer from the New Zealand Corps of Electrical and Mechanical Engineers. Ron had transferred from the Sultan's Armed Forces (SAF) and commanded the very efficient SSF workshops. Ron and Keith were both excellent additions to the SSF and brought a great deal of practical experience to the unit. Ron is now the New Zealand minister of defence and the minister of veterans' affairs – a very well-respected New Zealand senior politician.

The former Rhodesian officers brought their families to Oman. Married accommodation was not available to non-Omanis and Keith F was not prepared to organise any. They rented basic accommodation in Salalah for their families and they certainly added a healthy dimension to the unit by participating in mess functions.

However, eventually, they were replaced by Omanis; this had been the long-term plan all along, but it also seemed that Keith F was no longer comfortable with these 'intruders'. I do not think he was happy with those with an air of colonial independence and much preferred the compliant attitude of the former 22 SAS NCOs.

He informed the contract officers that the Palace Office – the unit's political guiding hand – no longer wanted non-UK passport holders in its ranks and that their contracts, when they expired, would not be renewed. I personally have my suspicions as to whether this edict had indeed come from the Palace Office. I took a certain amount of pleasure in reminding him that I was a UK passport holder. I don't believe these colonial non-Omanis were ever given the credit they deserved for the great deal they had contributed to the development and modernisation of the SSF based upon their extensive operational experience in the Rhodesian Special Forces, Vietnam and elsewhere.

———

I designed our motto, 'Swift and Deadly', as well as the D Squadron badge and the individually numbered special metallic badge awarded to SSF soldiers who had completed the D Squadron Counterterrorism (CT) course and continued to serve in the Squadron. This training involved Close Quarter Battle shooting; explosive demolition entry into buildings; assaulting buildings, aircraft and vehicles – and later maritime vessels; building abseiling skills; and fast-roping from helicopters. The motto and badges were soon approved by the Palace Office and Sultan Qaboos himself. I was very fortunate to have Captain Tony B as my second-in-command of D Squadron. Tony B had served in Oman with the SAS during the Dhofar War and was a very good Arabist. I had studied the language before joining SSF, and managed to get by, but never mastered writing it.

Under our command, D (Cobra) Squadron eventually became a very efficient counterterrorism organisation thanks to a huge amount of hard graft and relentless training. We became skilled in carrying out training in aircraft assaults, vehicle assaults and building assaults and we even progressed to maritime counterterrorism. We frequently travelled to Bahrain to train on Gulf Air aircraft and would spend several weeks in each year carrying out assaults on the various aircraft in their stable.

But training the counterterrorism team to always be ready to deploy into any situation was not without its hazards. For obvious reasons training had to be realistic and we spent a lot of time honing our close-quarters shooting and entry techniques. Explosives were used to gain entry to various buildings and structures. Unfortunately, during one training session, a squadron member got his timings wrong when he was attempting to gain entry into our 'bespoke' training facility and blew several fingers off his left hand. He was immediately given first aid and rushed off to the main hospital in Salalah. Keith F was observing this training session and decided to gather the somewhat shocked troops around him in the training room and give them a pep talk. His instincts were good; it was important, despite the awful accident, to stress the need for realistic training, and that in the event of an accident lessons needed to be learned to ensure it did not happen again. However, he could see that he was not getting through to the troops, who were looking more and more horrified with every passing second. As discreetly as possible I had to point out to him that, while giving his motivational speech, he was in fact standing on the injured man's detached fingers, which were poking out from under his desert boots.

On another occasion, Tony B and I were experimenting with various methods to clear reinforced glass from a window so that stun grenades could be thrown in or so that the assault team could effect entry. The method used was to place a detonator in a small explosive primer which was then placed at the end of a bent metal picquet. The detonator was connected by wire to a claymore firing device, a 'clacker'. I would creep up to the window, swing the pointed end of the piquet through the window, smashing the glass, and give the nod to Tony B behind me who would then detonate the explosive which would clear out the reinforced glass. Unfortunately, in this case the picquet bounced off the window and without getting the nod, Tony decided to blow the charge. KFB! I am still able to describe in detail all the colours of that explosion directly in front of me. It was some days before I recovered from the blast.

In 1987, I took a number of D Squadron officers and senior NCOs to visit the German counterterrorism team, GSG 9, based in Bonn. We spent a week or so training with them and comparing techniques. We carried out 'fast-roping' or 'swarming' from helicopters with them and we also learned the techniques for climbing tall apartment buildings on the outside using ladders to climb up from balcony to balcony – that was more than a little scary. GSG 9 had carried out a successful aircraft assault in Mogadishu in 1977. They are very professional and were extremely hospitable.

During the training we wore coveralls and World War II German parachute helmets – I wish I had kept one. At the end of our visit I was able to spend some time with the GSG 9 Commander Uwe Dee and I was privileged to receive an engraved GSG 9 Glock presentation dagger at the end of our visit. This now proudly hangs on my wall.

Following the visit to GSG 9 I was able to take my team to visit the counterterrorism team of 22 SAS in Hereford. We were hosted by B Squadron and carried out combined training and shooting with them. I was really pleased to be able to meet up with my former comrades again, especially Sailor, and several of them assisted us with the training. Interestingly, the training facilities in Hereford were no better than those of the SSF in Oman, but, of course, this was a UK Defence funding issue.

At the end of our visit we took the opportunity to visit Tony Fleming at his home in Hereford where he had returned after leaving the SSF some months earlier. He was a highly respected man amongst the SSF and it was a great pleasure to see him.

The training in maritime counterterrorism was carried out in the waters around Hong Kong and taught by the 'ninjas' of the Royal Hong Kong police maritime Special Duties Unit (SDU). Dhofaris are not particularly happy swimming in the sea, but by grim determination they soon learned the skills and techniques for assaulting ships at anchor, ships alongside and ships under way. One exercise in which we participated was against a cargo vessel out at sea and it took place shortly after a typhoon had swept the area. I have very clear memories of one of my Omani squad members using a jumar climbing system to scale a rope which, with a grapnel attached, had been fired onto the vessel from our following assault RIBs (rigid inflatable boats) by a compressed air Plummet gun. As he clung onto the rope hanging from the side of this giant ship a huge swell lifted the vessel, and its enormous, slowly turning propellers, some 12 feet out of the water and then another 12 feet down again, plunging the Omani deep into the water. He courageously continued his climb and threw down the caving ladder he had carried so the rest of us could climb up. I wanted to be the next onto the ship so my RIB closed up to the caving ladder which was, at its lowest point, some 4 feet in the air. I was held at the bow of our boat as it was thrown about and waited for an opportunity to jump and grasp the flailing ladder when it was closest to the sea. As I was being flung about I became aware of a pathetic sort of whimpering noise – I suddenly realised it was coming from me! Eventually I was able to jump and grasp the lowest rung and drag myself up onto the next rungs of the ladder. That was a long, exciting climb!

After the rest of the team had also scaled the ladder and the bridge had been secured we departed the vessel by jumping off the stern back into the giant sea. One minute I would be deep inside a huge hollow in the sea and the next moment I was perched on the top of a mountainous wave. We were relying on our wetsuits to keep us afloat until, eventually, we would each be found by the RIBs. I was incredibly proud of how we conquered our fears that day – myself included!

OPERATIONAL DUTIES AND LIFE IN OMAN

While those of us in D Squadron trained for counterterrorism operations, the desert Sabre squadrons trained for conventional warfare. But D Squadron was also responsible for carrying out discreet operations on behalf of the Oman Security Services (SIS). On one occasion I was contacted by SIS to say they had information that there was an arms cache located in the desert south or west of SOAF Thumrait airbase. Keith F was away on annual Christmas leave at the time, so I was in command of the regiment. A lot of operational incidents happened when he was away on leave and that pissed him off no end.

This was codenamed Operation *Thalib*. We analysed the information we were given, managed to locate where we believed the cache was most likely located and inserted a long-term OP. This was put in by the specialist 17 Troop of D Squadron and the operation was commanded on the ground by a very professional former SAS NCO, Jimmy S. During the operation the patrol had to cope with numerous camel spiders around their OP. The camel spider is a large carnivorous spider which injects a nerve-numbing liquid into its prey and then starts to devour the still-living flesh – frequently the faces of sleeping humans.

I coordinated all the aspects of the operation including the preparation of a quick reaction force (QRF) from the rest of D Squadron located back at the main base in Zeak. The whole operation had to be kept from the rest of the regiment, but members of the unit were used to 17 Troop disappearing on special tasks.

After a number of days with the 17 Troop operatives on the ground, it became obvious that the information was somewhat dated and that there were unlikely to be any potential terrorists coming to reclaim the cache. We then lifted the cache, which was contained in barrels in a cave complex, and took it back to the SSF base at Zeak. The equipment in the cache was extraordinary – there was a complete set of equipment with which to start a revolution! There were documents, leaflets, pamphlets, instruction books, explosives, weapons, mines, grenades, RPG-7s and silenced pistols. It was a veritable Aladdin's cave for sedition. The equipment had Soviet lettering, but the written matter was all in Arabic. The SIS 'spooks' were delighted with this find. We, of course, were disappointed that we were unable to ambush anybody coming to recover these items from the hide. I personally believe the hide had been there for some time and was left over from the Dhofar War. Regardless of its age, however, individuals could have created mayhem and murder with what was in that cache.

On his return from leave Keith F maximised the 'PR' aspects of 'his' operation and all the Omanis involved were given prestigious gallantry medals. Interestingly, but not surprisingly, the non-Omanis involved, myself and Jimmy S, were never mentioned at all.

But this is not to say that I didn't recognise the huge improvements the Jebali troops had made and I greatly enjoyed working with them; I found them keen to learn, and quick to acquire new skills. Like most mountain people they could take offence easily and tribal vendettas, especially blood vendettas, could continue generation after generation. They have an expression about their loyalties, 'Me against my brother; my brother and me against the tribe; the tribe against the world!' In a similar vein, I have heard other Omanis say about the Jebali, 'If you find a snake and a Jebali in your bed – throw out the Jebali first!' But I found them to be passionately loyal and courageous with a sense of humour.

They enjoy eating and talking and this is manifested in their *hafla*. This is a social get-together where a goat or several goats are roasted in a wood fire and a feast is enjoyed with animated conversations with everyone sitting on a mat around great mounds of meat and rice. I have fond memories of many such desert evenings.

Unlike the people, the climate and topography could take some time to get used to with the coastal fringe of Dhofar and Salalah affected by the winds of the south-west monsoon, known as the Khareef, between June and September. These surface winds encourage an upwelling of colder waters in the Indian Ocean which cool the overlying moisture-laden air. As this air is lifted over the jebel, the moisture condenses as thick, wet fogs over the hills.

During the Khareef, vision on the jebel is down to a few feet. Driving the steep, winding road from the jebel to Salalah and back became extremely hazardous. Each year there would be a number of fatalities as heavily-laden goods lorries travelling the 620 miles from Muscat would enter this wet, misty fog and lose control of their vehicles. The roads would be very slippery with a combination of spilled oil, diesel and water. In the SSF camp the rain-soaked buildings would become dark with mould and the camp would be swallowed up in the permanent white mist and fog. It was a surreal existence. However, only some 10 miles further north, where the jebel met the desert, the fog and rain would simply disappear and you would drive, as though through a curtain, into bright, blinding desert sunshine!

This rain and mist supports an annual regrowth of grass and trees over the following summer season. The Khareef brings nature to the barren hilltops and the brown hills start exploding into an emerald green carpet. Mile after mile of red barren-looking rocks and steep wadis become covered in new growth of grasses, bushes and trees.

During the later part of the Khareef, I would witness scores of storks assembling at a small lake near to the camp. They would noisily feed and prepare themselves for their long migrations from Europe to Africa. As the temperatures increased they would catch thermals and start spiralling up into the sky in ones and twos and then in larger groups and then finally the main body, with much squawking, would spiral their way high into the sky until they disappeared from view. One or two did not depart and would continue to stand beside the lake looking disconsolately skyward – they would fall prey to the various foxes and other predators that patrolled the desert.

The end of the Khareef would be a relief, even though the new growth was extraordinary to see – it was a claustrophobic time for everyone. It was possible to go a bit stir-crazy!

We were very lucky during my time in the SSF with two excellent British Regimental Medical Officers (RMO). The first one I served with was Tom Pollak who had a fascinating background. He was a fully qualified GP and had joined 10 Para, the reserve battalion of the Parachute Regiment, as a paratrooper. Tom was duly commissioned and soon became a major and company commander. He decided to attempt 22 SAS selection and passed with flying colours. But, because Tom was originally of Eastern European extraction he was not able to be security cleared. He offered to be the RMO for 22 SAS instead, but the same restrictions applied. Tom then joined the regular Parachute Regiment as a paratrooper and not surprisingly soon received a commission and joined me in 1 Para as my excellent second-in-command. Tom excelled at being a Parachute Regiment officer and as a doctor. So, I knew we were in safe hands when Tom was appointed as the SSF RMO.

But there was one incident when Tom's hands were not as safe as perhaps he would have liked them to be. The regiment was asked to go into some local villages in the area and shoot the feral dogs that were becoming dangerous. Tom was with a group from the SSF and, as a dog raced from behind a building, he opened fire with his shotgun. Unfortunately, a Pakistani administrative employee of the regiment had decided to follow a similar path to the dog and was hit in his rear end by some of Tom's pellets. The injured man let out a blood-curdling shriek and fell to the dirt. Mortified, Tom ran over to him, holding his smoking shotgun, and uttered the immortal words, 'Don't worry – I'm a doctor!'

Following Tom's return to the British Army, Ian P was appointed as our RMO, who had been the RMO at 22 SAS prior to joining the SSF. Ian was as competent as Tom but more of a cerebral individual. However, he was also always more than willing to make his views firmly known about medical matters even if they might conflict with those of Keith F. His outspoken manner did not appeal to everyone and as he had been the 22 SAS RMO it was difficult for anyone in the SSF, British or Omani, to pull the wool over his eyes. Ian eventually re-joined the British Army after leaving the SSF and became one of the most respected military psychiatrists in the army. He and I got on very well and I have remained very good friends with both him and Tom Pollak.

I would be sad to leave these new-found friends – British, Rhodesian, Jebali – but my three-year contract was up, and I had decided not to renew. I had enjoyed this adventure in Oman, the land of Sinbad the Sailor, but it was time for an entirely new chapter of my life to begin.

10

ROYAL ORDNANCE PLC; RELIANCE SECURITY LIMITED; TERRITORIAL ARMY, 1989-94

BECOMING A CIVILIAN

It seemed it was finally time to stop being a soldier. After leaving the SSF I returned to New Zealand, where my family had remained, and set about finding a new job. I had completed a number of correspondence courses while abroad but soon discovered there were very few job opportunities in New Zealand itself.

After a number of weeks of fruitless searching, I decided that I needed to look elsewhere for work, and so I travelled to the United Kingdom and stayed for some time at the Special Forces Club in the centre of London. I had been a member of this club since 1976 when I had first joined 22 SAS. I lived in the smallest room in the building; it was not cheap to live in London, but it gave me the opportunity to look for work in either military or security-based industries. I was eventually offered a job as a small arms sales manager with the Ammunition Division of Royal Ordnance, the British small arms manufacturer based at Royal Ordnance Factories (ROF) in Chorley, Lancashire. My salary interestingly was the same as I had been getting when I was with KMS in 1981, and this was now 1989! I moved to Chorley by myself initially, and then, six months later, my family, somewhat disheartened to have to leave behind friends and family in New Zealand, eventually joined me.

The Royal Ordnance Factories could trace their history right back to 1560 with the founding of the Royal Gunpowder Factory; now they were trying to find their way in an increasingly competitive marketplace under the ownership of British Aerospace (BAe). My initial role was selling small arms and support weapons ammunition; it was then expanded to include selling demolition explosives. One of the products I was involved in developing was 'frangible' ammunition. This small arms ammunition was designed to be used by counterterrorism forces in order to minimise the collateral damage that could be caused by a high-velocity round being fired into a street, in a building, on a vessel or in an aircraft. The project took me to a number of agencies including the SBS in Poole and the Irish Army in Dublin. Unfortunately, the ballistic characteristics of the round were inconsistent and so it was not a success.

I also travelled to potential clients to demonstrate an explosive called ECT or 'explosive cutting tape'. This is a very cleverly designed strip of adhesive explosive that is extremely useful for cutting through metal and small, specific areas. One interesting trip I made was a long arduous journey into Finland to a demolition range deep in the forests. I was tasked to demonstrate the use of ECT on German World War II aerial bombs so that they could be split open and the explosives inside safely be removed and destroyed. I believe they still had large stock piles of them left over from World War II. The bombs, less fuzes, were hung in a sling under a wooden frame; ECT was wrapped around them and detonated using a detonator and an electrical exploder. It was a very successful demonstration.

The main marketplaces for RO munitions were countries, frequently former British colonies, which still had UK military hardware such as 155mm and 105mm artillery as well as 30mm ammunition for the Aden cannon used in armoured vehicles and some aircraft.

I was able to expand my job and through promotion become an Ammunition Division international sales manager. This involved more travel, and I think I visited almost every country in Africa,

Asia, North America and Europe, with the obvious exception of the Soviet Union. Working for Royal Ordnance could certainly be quite testing and those of us working in sales often had an expression that Royal Ordnance could be almost guaranteed to 'snatch defeat from the jaws of victory'. I would often win an order, but the factory concerned was unable to fulfil the order in time or to the right specification; or to manufacture the quantity required; or to complete the order for any number of other reasons. The order was then lost to a competitor. It was a regular and frustrating experience.

During 1993 it was becoming obvious that RO was having difficulties in maintaining its sales world-wide against increasing competition from France, the United States, India and Pakistan. It was more and more difficult to get items produced on time to meet customers' requirements. In December 1995 I was called into an interview with the Director of Marketing, a corpulent former military brigadier, and advised that I was being made redundant. I was to be escorted to my desk and was required to leave the RO site within 20 minutes. This was not a total surprise to me as there had been redundancies announced in other departments over previous weeks and I was certainly an expensive commodity. What I did find totally unacceptable was the manner in which my redundancy was managed.

I stated quite firmly to this ex-brigadier that nobody was escorting me anywhere and that I would return to my desk, on my own, collect my personal items and then leave. On returning to my department I advised my colleagues and my assistants that I was leaving and wished them well. I had ridden to work on my Harley Davidson Sportster that morning and as I walked towards it in the carpark I thought, 'Do I turn right into ignominy or turn left and make my feelings about the manner of my departure apparent to all?' Right was towards the exit from the RO complex – left was towards the rather grand glass front doors of the RO headquarters. I fired up the Harley and turned left, riding through the two sets of glass sliding doors, then made a noisy, very noisy, victory lap around the lobby and vestibule of the headquarters complex. Then I turned right and finally departed from the clutches of RO and BAe.

I made a personal vow that, as soon as humanly possible, I would run my own company so that I could never be treated like that again. In hindsight, being made redundant was the best thing that could have happened to me!

However, at the time, it was a difficult financial situation to be in. I would need to find a job soon to make ends meet. I think I wrote some 500 or so letters applying for various vacancies in the United Kingdom and elsewhere. Replying to a letter is not a form of courtesy that is practised by many companies these days. The number of replies was small – so much so, that Cecilia and I called them GTFs – 'Get to Fuck' letters. We had to maintain a sense of humour and replies were grouped into good GTFs and bad GTFs. The difference being that some respondees actually said thank you for replying to their particular job vacancy!

Just after I arrived back in the United Kingdom to join RO in 1989 I had also applied to join the local Territorial Army (TA) unit which happened to be the Duke of Lancaster's Own Yeomanry. This was a UK-based Land Rover-borne reconnaissance unit specifically with an anti-Spetznaz (Russian Special Forces) role in the event of conflict with the Soviet Union. I thought my previous airborne and Special Forces experience would be useful in hunting down Spetznaz troops who might land in the United Kingdom. The Duke of Lancaster's Own Yeomanry had squadrons located throughout the Lancashire area and I worked with A Squadron, the Wigan-based squadron. I had had a little prior experience with the Territorial Army when I was a squadron commander with 21 SAS in London in 1981. This time I was to spend over ten years with the Territorial Army in various capacities before eventually retiring as a lieutenant colonel in 2000. The Duke of Lancaster's Own Yeomanry had its origins in the various troops of light horse raised in the eighteenth century in the county of

Lancaster. The sovereign holds the dukedom and has traditionally been the regiment's colonel-in-chief. At the loyal toast during a formal dinner officers of the regiment would say, 'Her Majesty, The Queen – The Duke of Lancaster'.

The regiment had a long and proud history. It had sent mounted infantry for service in the Anglo-Boer War as the Imperial Yeomanry, between 1900 and 1902. The Duke of Lancaster's Own Yeomanry also had a fascinating history as cavalry in World War I and was one of the last units to carry out a cavalry charge against an enemy. The unit continued to wear chain mail on the shoulders of formal dress in recognition of this fact. During World War II the regiment was mobilised as horsed cavalry but, in 1940, it converted into artillery and formed the 77th Medium and 78th Medium Regiments of Royal Artillery. The 78th went on to serve in Palestine, Syria and Italy as part of 6th Army Group, Royal Artillery.

The 77th remained in Northern Ireland until early 1944 when it prepared for the invasion of Europe. Landing in Normandy on D-Day plus 6, it was attached to 8th Army Group Royal Artillery and fought for the Odon Bridgehead and in the battle of the Falaise Gap. It also provided support for Operation *Market Garden* at Arnhem in September 1944.

In 1947 the Duke of Lancaster's Own Yeomanry was re-formed as an armoured regiment. Its role changed to reconnaissance in 1956, when it was equipped with armoured cars, but on 1 April 1967 it combined with the 40th/41st Royal Tank Regiment. Two years later, this combined regiment was reduced to a cadre until 1971 when it was re-formed as an infantry unit. On 1 April 1983, it re-joined the Royal Armoured Corps as a home defence reconnaissance unit equipped with Land Rovers. In other words, it changed from pumpkins to carrots to swedes to radishes then back to pumpkins again. On 1 November 1992 the regiment was eventually disbanded as a result of the Options for Change and its units amalgamated with The Queen's Own Mercian Yeomanry to form The Royal Mercian and Lancastrian Yeomanry with a 'D' (Duke of Lancaster's Own Yeomanry) Squadron.

But in 1989 it was still most definitely the Duke of Lancaster's Own Yeomanry, a regiment in its own right, and one I was proud to join as a major.

I could not have been more impressed by the hard graft that the Territorial Army soldiers whom I commanded put in week after week. As I've already mentioned, TA soldiers would work all week in various types of jobs – and at this point in time in the north-west of England the majority of these jobs would be extremely physically demanding – then on a Friday evening they would come into the drill hall and be fully prepared to spend an arduous weekend on exercise somewhere in the United Kingdom, before being back at their normal work first thing on a Monday morning.

Before the regiment was amalgamated I was promoted and posted as commanding officer of the 42 North West Brigade Specialist Training Team (BSTT). I was rebadged to SAS. The BSTT was based with the 42 Brigade Headquarters in Fulwood Barracks, Preston. These barracks were a fine example of a solid, grey, Victorian military fort. The BSTT was responsible for running all arms promotion and skills courses and my staff were all trained instructors from the various TA organisations located in the north-west of England. We were also responsible for organising and running shooting training for the brigade units as well as annual training exercises. This would result in a number of interesting exercises and courses, some in unusual places such as Russia and Hungary. Unfortunately, and somewhat remarkably, I was also injured more often than I ever was in the regular army, including sustaining a severed Achilles tendon on a United Nations military observers course in Russia and a badly fractured humerus after crashing my hang-glider on a military adventure training expedition in Spain.

Meanwhile back in the commercial world after several months job-hunting I was approached by Ken Holmes, a former Grenadier Guardsman and member of the Guards Independent Parachute

Squadron, to apply for the role of sales and marketing director with Reliance Aviation Security (RAS). I had first met Ken in Bahrain where he was the aviation security consultant with Gulf Air. Back then, of course, the SSF and I would frequently travel to Bahrain and train on Gulf Air aircraft. Ken was my point of contact there and we had always worked well together.

The company offices were near London Heathrow, with another smaller office in Crawley, near London Gatwick. During the week I stayed in a flat in Woking. The company provided security services to the airlines at both airports and so I got to know the M25 very well indeed, not to mention the M3 and M4 as I would make the lengthy journey home on a Friday night.

My role primarily involved growing the client base for RAS. It was a cut-throat business and competition was fierce. RAS was one of only four aviation security companies licensed by the British Aviation Authorities to work in London Heathrow and one of three licensed to work in Gatwick. Aviation companies were experts at playing one security company off against another. It was long, stressful hours and a real learning curve but with excellent employers from whom I learned a great deal. There were also some unexpected upsides.

One particular day in 1993, I was required to personally supervise the security at the British Midland hangar at London Heathrow. Richard Branson was naming his new Airbus A340-300 aircraft and he was going to call the aircraft 'Lady in Red'. He had contacted Buckingham Palace and requested that Diana, Princess of Wales, personally name and christen the new aircraft. She duly arrived in the hangar and, as she was about to name the aircraft with the traditional bottle of champagne, a scissor-hoist at the side of the aircraft which had been concealed by an awning started rising and on it, seated behind his grand piano, was Chris De Burgh, singing his hit song 'Lady in Red', much to the great delight of Her Royal Highness.

On 9 March 1994 I had more than my fair share of my 15 minutes of fame. The IRA fired four mortar bombs from a car parked in the Excelsior Hotel car park beside Heathrow Airport.

This car park was right beside the airport perimeter. The bombs, which did not explode, landed near the northern runway. I was interviewed by a BBC camera crew at the time and mentioned that I had carried out a recent security survey of the hotel and had identified the Excelsior Hotel car park as a potential mortar attack site. So started a fascinating circus of interviews, both radio and television, and I was passed from one media provider to the next with interviews all around London. The furore only lasted for about two or three days and it was a whirlwind while it happened. I even had a call from relations in New Zealand who had seen me being interviewed on CNN.

In 1995 RAS was sold to ICTS, an Israeli security company, and I took over Reliance Security's manned guarding operation based in Crawley. Man-guarding is even more cut-throat than aviation security. It did not take me long to decide that this wasn't for me and I put in a request to Reliance Security to work three days a week while I established my own security consultancy business. They kindly agreed and while they were looking for a full-time replacement for me they were happy for us to continue together, while I would tried to obtain new clients for my own consultancy in the two days that I wasn't working for Reliance.

Overall, I had learned how to successfully operate a business on tight profit margins for demanding clients while also trying to both train and retain the best people for the job. On the side I had also begun studying for my Master's in Security Management. Now it was clearly time for me to strike out fully on my own.

11

AMA ASSOCIATES LIMITED; TERRITORIAL ARMY; AND A RETURN TO NEW ZEALAND, 1994–PRESENT

Once my notice with Reliance Security was completed I became an independent security consultant and established AMA Associates Ltd. The early years were very lean as I tried to establish a client base and I spent a lot of time travelling the country doing surveys and working long hours often in obscure places. Yet, strangely, in many ways it was as if my life had gone full circle and many of the places I visited reminded me of my far-off, younger days.

Initially, I set up the company office in the house and one of the rooms was set aside for the production of training manuals and training pamphlets. I used many Special Forces colleagues whom I knew and I also worked on the grandfather principle – if I didn't know an individual I would only employ them if they were known to somebody I knew and trusted.

As my company gained more contracts I was able with the assistance of Mick 'Joda' R to put in a bid for surveillance training for the Department of Work and Pensions (DWP). Mick was former Parachute Regiment and I had first met him when I joined 3 PARA in 1973. He was serving with 22 SAS at that time. He then worked with the 'Det' in Northern Ireland. He was the most amazing surveillance operator and he could make himself invisible in a crowd or an empty street! He is truly one of the best surveillance operatives I've ever worked with.

We won the contract and ran surveillance courses all over the United Kingdom and Northern Ireland for DWP field staff. I also continued to run training courses to qualify aviation staff in all aspects of aviation security as well as carrying out air cargo security assessments. Also at this stage, the International Maritime Organisation (IMO) was developing a security regime for ports and ships and so I became qualified to run ship security officer and port security officer courses.

Two major tasks developed as a result of these aviation and maritime courses. The first was to prepare a security assessment for all of Egypt's airports. I travelled the length and breadth of Egypt generally by commercial aircraft but also by railway. It was an arduous project but a most interesting experience. A number of airports were beside the most amazing archaeological ruins from Ancient Egypt. As a very small boy in Egypt I had visited the pyramids and the Cairo Museum where I stood staring, transfixed, at the skeletal feet of King Tutankhamun, which had become exposed from his shroud. I felt very fortunate indeed to be able to see these ancient wonders of the world once again.

The second was to deliver port security training courses to Sri Lankan port security executives and then to carry out an assessment of all of Sri Lanka's ports' security in order to have their maritime insurance liabilities re-assessed by Lloyds of London. At that time Sri Lanka was required to pay extremely high maritime insurance premiums because of the actions of the Tamil Tigers, an extremely militant and violent secessionist movement, especially their maritime attack units – the Sea Tigers. By this point the Sea Tigers had already sunk some 29 Sri Lankan naval patrol boats and even a freighter.

Once again, I was ably assisted by Mike R, my fellow troop commander in 22 SAS, in this work and we would make several trips to the country until a change in government meant a change in business relationships. Driving around Sri Lanka reminded me very much of my days growing up in the mid-1950s in Singapore and Malaya, watching immaculately dressed schoolchildren emerging from the depths of the jungle to await their school bus, just as they had decades before, and I greatly enjoyed my time there making many Sri Lankan friends along the way.

One of my most challenging early projects took place in Kiev, in Ukraine, then still part of the Soviet Union. I was required to carry out a security assessment for a new building project. I suspect it was going to be occupied by a Russian oligarch or a member of the Russian mafia because the level of protection was quite extraordinary, including protecting against vehicle bombs, RPG 7 rockets and snipers! I worked with Mike 'Bugsy' M on this project. Bugsy was former Parachute Regiment and had also served with the 'Det'. His expertise was anti-bugging and he would make sure that no devices had been left in any of the buildings that were being constructed. Amongst the rubble disturbed when the buildings were being constructed we came across quite a few World War II artefacts, such as Wehrmacht helmets.

Kiev had a huge war memorial situated on the banks of the Dnieper River and dominating this memorial was a massive titanium statue of a woman holding a drawn sword pointed towards Moscow in 'Mother Russia'. Each of the capitals of the countries that constituted the Soviet Union had an identical titanium statue pointing towards Moscow. The Kiev War Memorial predominately commemorated the fierce fighting that took place in Kiev and along the Dnieper during World War II. The museum certainly brought home the massive scale of the fighting that had occurred. However, there was also a section of the memorial devoted to the Russian incursion into Afghanistan. I was particularly struck by the photos of the young conscript soldiers taken in Afghanistan which could easily have been photos of young American, Australian or Kiwi soldiers such as myself, in Vietnam.

In 2001 the BP Algeria security contract in Algeria was due for renewal. This contract involved providing security teams to protect the desert drilling stations and BP's main desert bases. Working together with former RMP Mike Lord and his company, we prepared a very competitive quote and our bid was successful.

I've always had an interest in visiting Algeria from reading Jean Paul Lartéguy's books about the French Paras and 'Le Légion' fighting in Vietnam and Algeria – *The Centurions*, *The Praetorians* and *The Bronze Drums*. Similarly, it was another dangerous time to be in the capital city, Algiers, as well as in the surrounding towns. Extremists were carrying out brutal terror attacks on their own population as well as against 'foreigners'. A specialty involved setting up a false road block, a *'faux barrage'*, disguised as the police or the army. Civilians were ambushed and murdered at these roadblocks and normally had their throats cut. This was meant to indicate that the person who is murdered is less worthy than an animal. This type of murder was called having a Kabila smile – a town where many of these killings were carried out.

Throughout the course of the work for BP I visited Algeria a number of times. It is a vast country of desert. Flying over the great tracts of gravelly sand in the vast hinterland I could see the tyre tracks and seismic explosion holes from explorations made in the 1930s clear and fresh as the day they were made.

Movement for BP personnel through Algiers was highly protected with armed guards accompanying each vehicle convoy to and from airports and into hotel grounds that were as heavily guarded as military bases. Vehicle travel was done at high speed with the locally employed guards waving pistols and AK-47s out of the car windows shouting at cars that did not move aside quickly enough. All of these locally contracted guards had their precious Ray Ban sunglasses. One day I watched with amusement when one of the security guards was shouting at a civilian car as we passed and as he looked back to give a final glower at the car's occupants the slipstream caught his Ray Bans, which promptly took flight, to be crushed by the following vehicle. His look of despair was a picture to behold.

In Algiers and in the desert, I met a number of friends and colleagues from my military days. These included Pete McAleese, with whom I had served in South Africa and who was now providing close protection at a villa in Algiers, and 'Minky' M from 8 Troop, B Squadron days, who was providing security for clients in the Algiers Sofitel hotel. I guess we were all doing exactly what we were good at.

———

While working hard to establish my business, I continued with my Territorial Army commitments, commanding the 42 Brigade Specialist Training Team (BSTT) based in Fulwood Barracks in Preston, Lancashire. One of the international military exercises I participated in with the Territorial Army was called Partnership for Peace and it was held in Hungary. We were based in a military camp near Lake Balaton.

Historically, Lake Balaton was the location of Operation *Spring Awakening*. This was the last major German offensive launched during World War II and was begun in great secrecy by the Germans on 6 March 1945. They launched attacks near Lake Balaton, an area which included some of the last oil reserves still available to the Axis Forces. The operation involved many German units withdrawn from the failed Ardennes Offensive on the Western Front, including the 6th SS Panzer Army and the 1st SS Panzer Division, Leibstandarte SS Adolf Hitler (LSSAH). Almost inevitably, the operation was an abject failure. Despite early gains, the operation was a perfect example of Hitler's increasingly poor military judgement towards the end of the war. Its chief flaw was that the offensive was far too ambitious in scope, and the operation failed just ten days after its launch.

The participants in 'Partnership for Peace' were all NATO members. There were military units from each participating country and each of these countries had a small headquarters, commanded by a lieutenant colonel and comprising a small staff. In this exercise we worked through a number of scenarios, with each participant contributing an overview of how its national resources could be utilised and could contribute to the big picture.

Inevitably, there were some amusing incidents. It became very noticeable to everyone that the French commanding officer could barely tolerate the commanding officer of the British unit participating in the exercise – the Royal Regiment of Fusiliers. This regiment's headdress is a dark-blue beret with a white hackle with a red top. This strained atmosphere went on for a number of days until a social evening when, after a few drinks, the French commanding officer exploded, pointed to the beret and hackle of the British commanding officer and said in tones of horror and with his very own Peter Sellers accent, 'I know the 'eeestory of your ploome!', and stood almost trembling with passion in front of the fusilier. It seems that in the 1800s this British regiment had soundly defeated a French force and the British soldiers as they advanced over the battlefield had dipped their white hackles in the blood of dead Frenchmen. Who said time heals?

After the exercise, we were all invited to attend a number of Hungarian cultural events at a small village on the outskirts of Budapest. The Hungarians are great horsemen and we were all seated in a small wooden stand watching a terrific display of riding and individual horsemanship. As we sat there, it became increasingly obvious that a considerable fire had started in a village behind the display with flames appearing as well as great columns of black smoke. One of the British NCOs leaned over to his German counterpart and quipped, 'Just like when you were here last time?' He got a wry smile in return.

Following the end of the Cold War, we began to run exercises in conjunction with Russian forces, rather than casting them in the role of the enemy. In February 1996 I was selected to attend a four-week United Nations military observers (UNMO) course at the Russian Vystral Higher Military Academy in Solnechnorgorsk which was located about 44 miles north of Moscow.

The Vystral Academy is over 100 years old and is an all arms training facility. On the course were two other British officers, ten Russian officers from all three services, and two US Special Forces officers, both of whom were Russian speakers. Most of the Russians had served in Afghanistan and a number had also served in Chechnya.

The training was very detailed, but the presentation skills and equipment were dated and items such as stationery were in short supply. The weather was very, very cold – minus 20 degrees

Celsius – and it brought home to me how difficult it would have been to fight in such freezing temperatures.

The directing staff was also from the three services and had served in most communist-sponsored countries in the world. The chief instructor, Lieutenant Colonel Potcharev, an army man, soon established that he and I had been serving in the town of Ongiva in Angola at the same time – but on opposite sides!

Unfortunately, one week from the end of the course I severed my Achilles tendon during a vigorous game of mini football. I was not prepared to leave the course, so I had a taped up 'floppy foot' for the final exercise. During this exercise our 'opponents' were a company of Russian paratroopers. At one stage they 'invaded' the UNMO base and dragged several of us down some metal stairs and into waiting BMP armoured vehicles. I could see they thought I was weak as I grimaced each time my injured Achilles tendon took a hammering. Needless to say, the day after I arrived back in the UK I was on the operating table having the tendon repaired.

At the end of the course we were formally presented with our UNMO badges and certificates, but the badges had to be collected from the bottom of a blue UN helmet which, of course, was filled with vodka!

In May 1997 I was commissioned to carry out a 'value for money assessment' of the US $36 million contract signed between the government of Papua New Guinea and the private military company Sandline International for the provision of military services to assist in the 'neutralisation' of the Bougainville Resistance Army (BRA), a secessionist movement. I was asked to carry out this task by 'Cush' C, a good friend and highly experienced and respected former Senior NCO in 22 SAS. Cush and I had worked together in 22 SAS and we have always been a good team. We both knew Tim Spicer, a former Scots Guards officer and, in my opinion, an SAS 'wannabe'. I also knew JN van der Bergh, a fellow paratrooper from my days in the SADF, and now a senior member of Sandline, which was a South African

PMC. Spicer and Sandline had worked together in Sierra Leone providing 'approved' support for the embattled government there. This had caused the UK Government some embarrassment because the use by them of a PMC was not widely known.

We were tasked to carry out this assessment by a client on behalf of the government of Papua New Guinea with terms of reference provided by the Attorney General, Mr Sao R Gabi.

As part of the project we were required to analyse the 'Top Secret' contract signed by the government representative, the Hon CS Haiveta MP and Spicer himself, witnessed by Mr Veleiamo, Acting Deputy Secretary and JN van der Bergh respectively.

The background to this major contract was that, in 1989, local landowners had shut down the Bougainville Pangura copper mine to simultaneously protest against the environmental destruction it caused and demand independence. In 1996, with promising peace initiatives having failed to yield results, a major military offensive against the BRA having achieved little, and a national election imminent, Prime Minister Julius Chan was persuaded to agree to a covert contract with Sandline International. This contract involved Sandline personnel and the Papua New Guinea Defence Force working together in an operation called 'Project Contravene' designed to defeat the rebel forces and recapture Bougainville. In February 1997, the government, which had received about 44 per cent of its revenue from the copper mine, agreed to pay Sandline International US $36 million with an initial payment of $18 million.

The head of the Defence Force, Major General Jerry Singirok, was having misgivings about the political impact of such a military operation by January 1987, and, in particular, about putting defence force personnel under the command of foreign mercenaries. In February 1997 the details of 'Project Contravene' became public with the use of Sandline International and the dubious financial arrangements for funding the project coming under widespread condemnation both in Papua New Guinea and overseas. As a result, the project abruptly ended.

Our conclusion, after analysing and assessing the various commercial documents, was that the cost of equipment supplied by Sandline was fair and reasonable; the personnel costs were excessive; and the plan submitted by Spicer and Sandline was fundamentally flawed.

In 1999, an international arbitration commission and an Australian court ruled that the Papua New Guinea government must make the payment to Sandline. The size of the payment, and what proportion of Sandline's US $18 million claim it represents, were not made clear.

The Papua New Guinea government has since reached a ceasefire agreement with the BRA.

Tim Spicer would later surface in Afghanistan, when his new company, Aegis Defence Services, was awarded a US $293 million contract to coordinate all the security for Iraqi reconstruction projects. Under this 'cost-plus' contract, the military covered all of the company's expenses, plus a pre-determined percentage of whatever they spent, which critics said was a licence to over-bill.

In 2011, Tim Spicer and Aegis were awarded a US $497 million contract by the US State Department to assume security force operations at the US Embassy in Kabul, Afghanistan which, depending on your viewpoint, goes some way to proving either that 'You can't keep a good man down' or 'You can fool some of the people all of the time'.

In AMA I had avoided becoming involved in PMC work. I felt that it was a 'meat market' and most companies worked hard at obtaining operatives at the lowest price possible in order to maximise their profit. I watched as highly trained Special Forces operatives were replaced by former UK line infantry soldiers, then by Gurkhas, then by former SADF personnel and finally by commercially trained civilians. It was certainly a lucrative market but not for my company.

In December 1999 I was invited by friend and fellow Parachute Regiment officer Simon B to join a battlefield tour of Vietnam. We had served together in 3 Para. This visit was the first ever foreign battlefield tour of Vietnam sanctioned by the Vietnamese government. Also on the tour to keep a close eye on the administration was RSM Andy Gough, whom I was pleased to see again. He had been one of my NCOs in 1 Para. His inimitable good humour would prevail throughout the battlefield tour despite the best the communist officials could throw at us. I jumped at this chance to revisit Vietnam and I also enjoyed the opportunity to brief my touring colleagues on the role of the ANZAC forces in what is called the 'American War'.

The aim of the tour was to study all the aspects of the wars in Indochina since 1945 in order to learn lessons relevant to the conduct of military operations. The tour was carried out from north to south. The French Indochina War was studied in detail at Dien Bien Phu and then we moved south to cover the American War in Hue and around Ho Chi Minh City (Saigon) to include ANZAC operations. We spent two days in Hanoi and visited the various war museums around the city as well as visiting the infamous 'Hanoi Hilton' where US prisoners of war were imprisoned. Jane Fonda visited this prison when she was carrying out her visit to Hanoi during the War and where she earned the permanent abhorrence of Vietnam veterans, including me, and gained herself the epithet 'Hanoi Jane'. When she met several PoWs they gave her notes to take home to their families – Fonda gave these to the North Vietnamese and her actions resulted in several US PoWs being severely beaten and tortured.

The French influence was very obvious in Hanoi with wide boulevards and lakes in the city centre. Also obvious were the B52 bomb craters around the bridges crossing the Red River and now used as duck ponds by local farmers.

While in Hanoi I was able to meet up with Neil Shrimpton with whom I had worked in Phnom Penh, Cambodia when I was involved in a demining project recce for BAe. He was now the BAe agent in Hanoi. He took me out one afternoon for a 'special treat'. The treat involved a long ride on the back of separate mopeds to a small restaurant on the outskirts of Hanoi. At the restaurant, as an honoured guest and Vietnam War veteran, I was given the still beating heart of a cobra immersed in a glass of the cobra's blood and fiery rice wine to consume! The cobra was eviscerated in front of me and then it was deep fried as part of the meal that followed. Some treat!

After a short 40-minute flight from Hanoi we landed at Dien Bien Phu where the French Army base was overwhelmed by the Viet Minh and surrendered on 7 May, 1954. The first thing that strikes you is the flatness of the valley bottom in which the town sits; it is completely overlooked from all sides. The airfield is in the same place but is longer than it was in 1954 and is now paved. Little has changed since the battles there although there are more houses made of concrete instead of bamboo. Many of the French hill positions such as *Beatrice, Gabrielle* and *Elaine* are still well preserved with obvious trench lines and bunkers but, interestingly, very few craters from the furious artillery bombardment they received during the battles. The hulks of the French M24 tanks and many of their guns remain where they were when the French surrendered. A difficult two-hour drive into the mountains north-west of Dien Bien Phu takes you to the Viet Minh General Giap's headquarters hidden in thick jungle and the return journey shows just how much the surrounding hills completely dominated the French Army positions in the valley below. In the evenings of our stay I would walk around the airstrip and you could sense the spirits of the French soldiers and their allies and the Viet Minh who died there. One evening beside the airstrip I picked up a souvenir of my visit – a fist-sized shard of shrapnel that had been lying in the dirt for 45 years.

From Dien Bien Phu we travelled to Hue, the ancient capital of Vietnam. We were fortunate to have with us a former US Marine Corps (USMC) officer, Tom Eagan, who had been involved with the vicious street fighting around Hue during the Tet Offensive in 1968. Hue is a built-up area astride the Perfumed River and it is dominated by its massive citadel surrounded by canals. The Viet Cong and North Vietnamese forces took and held the citadel for 25 days and its recapture produced some of the most sustained fighting of the American War. When they captured the citadel the North Vietnamese forces massacred over 3,000 of the city's residents who were considered 'enemies of the people' – these included schoolteachers, doctors and intellectuals. Their bodies were later found hastily buried in the sandhills surrounding the city. Most of the fighting in and around Hue involved the USMC with the 1st US Air Cavalry fighting in the surrounding areas as the North Vietnamese and the Viet Cong tried to withdraw from the city. At one stage we walked from our hotel to the Perfumed River, a trip that took us 15 minutes – in 1968 it had taken the USMC five days to fight along the same distance. In a small museum was one of the main weapons used by the USMC for street fighting, the Ontos light tank. This vehicle carried six 106mm recoilless rifles and was, in fact, a giant multi-barrelled shotgun.

We went to Ho Chi Minh City (HMC) from Hue. HMC, or Saigon as many of the residents still call it, is much bolder and brassier than Hanoi. It still retains its air of independence despite now being communist. There is even still a Hard Rock Café there. From HMC we visited the tunnels of Cu Chi which have become a bit of a theme park with special 'wide' tunnels for the 'larger' foreign tourist. One has to respect those from both sides who fought each other in this subterranean darkness. We also set out to visit the former ANZAC fire support base, FSB Coral. The defence of Coral was over a three-week period (12 May–6 June, 1968) and although hard fought was a success for the ANZAC troops. Unfortunately, despite having several GPS and numbers of maps of that era we were not able to exactly locate where the battles had taken place. Nature had gently removed any remaining signs.

It was an interesting experience for me being back in Vietnam some 40 years after I had fought in its jungles as a young platoon commander. I did get a little tired at each museum we visited of being constantly reminded of the war crimes of 'the US and its running dogs' without, surprise, surprise, any mention of the barbarity of the North Vietnamese against the civilians of the South – some of which I had seen for myself. It was also tiring being regaled with the most fantastic tales of bravery and heroism by North Vietnamese soldiers (the Viet Cong were hardly mentioned).

However, the Vietnamese we met, other than officials, were friendly and helpful and very interested in our visit. It must be remembered that since fighting the French, the US and its allies, the Vietnamese have had a major war with China and they also invaded Cambodia, destroying the dreadful regime of Pol Pot and the Khmer Rouge. Several times Vietnamese told me that their country's sacrifices in destroying the Khmer Rouge had never been internationally recognised.

My last view of Vietnam as we flew out of HMC's airport, the former massive US airbase at Ton San Nhut, was a huge pile of broken transport and fighter aircraft from the 'American War', all lying on top of each other as though they had been swept there by a giant broom.

My Territorial Army duties as well as my full-time work kept me busy, but I also served as a local magistrate for seven years, hearing cases from the Family and Youth Courts. However, I still wanted to stretch myself mentally, so while still working I committed to completing my Master's degree in Security Management at the University of Leicester in 1996. I had always been conscious throughout my military service and then in civilian life that I did not have tertiary education qualifications. In all honesty, I had simply not been interested after secondary school and then I became a full-time operational soldier with no time for such 'luxuries'. Once I entered the commercial marketplace, however, I soon realised that tertiary qualifications were invaluable in convincing potential civilian employers that I was not some loud-mouthed ex-army stereotype who only got things done by abusing and pressurising his staff. I so enjoyed my Master's that I eventually committed to pursuing a doctorate degree through the Centre for Defence and Security Studies at the University of Lancaster under the tutelage of the centre's head, Dr Martin Edmondson. Appropriately for me, the focus of my doctorate was on the effectiveness of 22 SAS as an extension of successive British governments' foreign and defence policies between 1950 and 2000. I successfully defended my thesis in 2005 but the subject focus caused quite a few headaches over at the Ministry of Defence and especially UK Special Forces

Headquarters. When the thesis was eventually published, in the form of a book, after having gone through the torturous Ministry of Defence approval process, I was still banned from visiting any UK Special Forces locations for five years.

But Cecilia and I were simply too busy to experience any angst as a result of this decision. Any free moment we had we were travelling and exploring. We particularly enjoyed a trip down memory lane travelling through southern Africa where I celebrated my 50th birthday with a bungee jump off Victoria Falls. It was an interesting sensation, a bit like a terminal freefall, except for the spinning once the 'bounces' had finished. The spinning seemed to go on for a very long time despite the fact that I had my arms outstretched!

In 2000 Cecilia had been diagnosed with breast cancer and, despite periods of remission, in 2004 it had returned. We decided that this was now a good time for us to return to New Zealand and for her to have her treatment there. We had lived away since 1989 and as both our children were grown up and had moved out of home it was time for us to move on too.

I sold AMA Associates, ensuring that all my operatives had security of tenure for at least 12 months, and sold the house; and in late November 2005 Cecilia and I moved back to New Zealand to live in a house in the beautiful Marlborough Sounds which we had bought back in 2000.

I had been born in Dover but, since 1959, New Zealand had been my adopted home. Cecilia was a fourth-generation New Zealander, so she was thrilled to be home and surrounded by friends and family.

The year after we arrived was the New Zealand 'Year of the Veteran' – a government initiative to recognise military veterans and their service to the country. I wanted to contribute so I organised the 'Ride of the Veterans'. This was a motorcycle odyssey around all the Returned Servicemen's Association (RSA) clubs throughout New Zealand with the aim of collecting donations for the Vietnam Veterans' Children's and Grandchildren's fund – The Wallace Foundation.

I invited Dave Barr from the United States to join me on this ride. Dave is, of course, the US Marine Vietnam and Pathfinder veteran who was severely injured during the Bush War when his vehicle went over a mine and who was rescued from the destroyed and blazing vehicle by Colonel Jan Breytenbach. Dave became a double leg amputee but rather than complain about his new disability he became a world champion for the Leonard Cheshire VC Homes for the Disabled. Dave rode his old Harley Davidson motorcycle through almost every country in the world including Siberia and China highlighting the plight of the disabled and achieving a number of Guinness World Records at the same time.

After his injury I had seen Dave again for the first time six years later when he visited Cecilia and me in the United Kingdom. He arrived at our house and said, in his southern drawl, 'Sir, I need to apologise to you'. I asked him what for. He replied, 'I am sorry I did not kill that terr!' Years before, when we were on operations together in southern Angola, Dave had gone outside our patrol perimeter to answer the call of nature. He had his rifle in his left hand and a combat shovel in his right hand. Several yards out into the veldt he and a SWAPO operative caught sight of each other at exactly the same time. They then both rapidly withdrew in opposite directions as quickly as possible. When he reached the safety of our perimeter I asked him what had happened. He explained to me the circumstances and I asked, 'Did you kill him?' When he answered in the negative I, apparently, turned on my heels and walked away. This had been on Dave's conscience for all these years. This man is a true warrior!

We had remained good friends ever since and it was a real pleasure to have him along for this ride. Also riding with us were two other Kiwi Vietnam veterans, John Coleman, a veteran of Whiskey 3 Company tour, and Bruce Gordon, who had served with me in Vietnam. Later in our trip we were joined by a senior member of the NZSAS. The trip was a great opportunity to visit the length and breadth of New Zealand while contributing to a worthy charity. Through the generosity of everyday men and women we were able to donate some $50,000 New Zealand dollars to the Vietnam Veterans Children's and Grandchildren's fund.

Riding with Dave Barr was an experience for us all. I had provided him with a 1200cc Harley Davidson Sportster and the only alteration he had to do was to add an additional strong spring on to the brake pedal to compensate for the fact that his right foot was permanently resting on this brake. We all finished this four-week journey with the greatest respect and admiration for Dave. He is the most committed and determined individual I have ever known.

Now I am back in New Zealand permanently I am able to attend our Vietnam Victor 5 Company reunions. These are held every two years. Our numbers are growing smaller, through age and illness, but we still have a relatively large cohort enhanced by many wives and families who also attend.

These reunions are always memorable with so many true, and somewhat embellished, tales of derring-do shared with much laughter! However, I always dread the moment when one of my platoon comrades-in-arms approaches me, beer in hand, and says with a wicked grin, 'You never knew this, Boss, but ...'. I then hear about some mischievous event that took place in Vietnam of which, I am pleased to say, I was totally unaware at the time.

On our return to New Zealand Cecilia had entered the local cancer programme and started chemotherapy as her cancer was again active. Only those who have been involved with the dreadful process of hospital visits, tests, high points and inevitable low points will understand our journey. We had held each other in hospital car parks in the United Kingdom and now New Zealand as we wept together after sessions with kind but ultimately powerless medical specialists.

The following 12 months in New Zealand with my dear wife are memories that I do not wish to share but in September 2007 she died in my arms at our house in Tara Bay. Our children were with us.

In her memory I have ensured that I have not dulled my sense of adventure. In 2014 I travelled to the US to join a group of motorcycling 21 SAS 'blades' (operatives) who were going to travel the length of Route 66. I did not know any of them although we all had the common link of having served in 21 SAS at some point. We travelled some 2,500 miles together from Boston to Los Angeles. I had missed the 'black' humour of the military since returning to New Zealand and it was a thoroughly enjoyable experience being part of it again. The quips, insults and having the 'piss' taken constantly – the caustic wit of these centurions is to be enjoyed in a way that only a soldier would understand.

I travelled the world witnessing the ordinary man, politicians, kings and princes at their best and at their worst. I have fought beside and against many exceptional soldiers. Commitment, integrity, honesty and preparedness are essential ingredients for the Universal Soldier and I have shared my journey with some of the best. The warrior, the Pilgrim who goes 'always a little further', is indeed a driven man but following the 'road to Samarkand' will always have its price. Would I do it all again? In a heartbeat!

INDEX